SpringerBriefs in Latin American Studies

More information about this series at http://www.springer.com/series/14332

Julie Cupples · Kevin Glynn

Shifting Nicaraguan Mediascapes

Authoritarianism and the Struggle for Social Justice

CLAG
clagscholar.org

Springer

Julie Cupples
Institute of Geography, School of GeoSciences
University of Edinburgh
Edinburgh
UK

Kevin Glynn
Department of Geography and Environmental Sciences
Northumbria University
Newcastle upon Tyne
UK

ISSN 2366-763X ISSN 2366-7648 (electronic)
SpringerBriefs in Latin American Studies
ISBN 978-3-319-64318-2 ISBN 978-3-319-64319-9 (eBook)
https://doi.org/10.1007/978-3-319-64319-9

Library of Congress Control Number: 2017947468

Printed on acid-free paper

This Springer imprint is published by Springer Nature
The registered company is Springer International Publishing AG
The registered company address is: Gewerbestrasse 11, 6330 Cham, Switzerland

Colonos are kidnapping, killing and raping indigenous peoples.
Source La Prensa (Zoad Mendoza 2016).
Photograph reproduced with permission of *La Prensa*

Acknowledgements

Special thanks to our collaborators and wider research community in Nicaragua, in particular Dixie Lee and Alta Hooker at URACCAN, Irving Larios at INGES, the Communal Creole government of Bluefields, and the staff of CEJUDHCAN. Thanks to all the Costeño broadcasters, activists, civil society leaders and intellectuals who made time for us over the past decade, especially Margarita Antonio, Deborah Bush, Shaun Bush, Avelino Cox, Raúl Davies, Juan Herbacio, Dolene Miller and Nora Newball. We are also grateful to Sofía Montenegro for sharing her insights on the Nicaraguan mediascape with us and to the editors of *La Prensa* and *Confidencial* for giving us permission to republish some of their photos. Thanks also to the Nicaraguans who share extensively on social media, enabling us to continue our fieldwork even when we are not in the 'field'.

We also wish to thank the Marsden Fund of the Royal Society for substantial research funding (grant number MAU1108, Geographies of Media Convergence 2013–2016) that has enabled us to do most of the fieldwork and conference dissemination on which this project depends.

Earlier versions of this work have been presented in various forums, including the Department of Geography at the London School of Economics, the Nature Culture symposium at the Institute of Latin American Studies, University of London, the annual conference of the Association of American Geographers in San Francisco, Victoria University of Wellington and Otago University. We would like to thank the people who made these presentations possible, including Alice Beban, Tony Binns, Ryan Centner, Gareth Jones, Sara Keene, Marcela Palomino and Francesca Zunino.

Special thanks also to Tom Slater, a dear friend and colleague, for encouraging us to think through the lens of agnotology.

Contents

Abbreviations

BCN	Banco Central de Nicaragua—Nicaraguan Central Bank
CALPI	Centro de Asistencia Legal para los Pueblos Indígenas—Legal Assistance Centre for Indigenous Peoples
CEJIL	Centro por la Justicia y el Derecho Internacional—Center for Justice and International Law
CEJUDHCAN	Centro de Justicia y Derechos Humanos de la Costa Atlántica de Nicaragua—Centre of Justice and Human Rights of the Atlantic Coast of Nicaragua
CENIDH	Centro Nicaragüense de Derechos Humanos—Nicaraguan Centre for Human Rights
CEPREV	Centro para la Prevención de la Violencia—Centre for the Prevention of Violence
CONADETI	Comisión Nacional de Demarcación y Titulación—National Commission for Demarcation and Titling
CONAIE	Confederación de Nacionalidades Indígenas del Ecuador—Confederation of Indigenous Nationalities of Ecuador
CPC	Consejo de Poder Ciudadano—Council of Citizen Power
ERM	Environmental Resources Management
ESIA	Environmental and Social Impact Assessment
FSLN	Frente Sandinista para la Liberación Nacional—Sandinista Front for National Liberation
GRACCN	Gobierno Regional de la Región Autónoma de la Costa Caribe Norte—Regional Government of the Autonomous Region of the North Caribbean Coast
GTRK	Gobierno Territorial Rama-Kriol—Rama-Kriol Territorial Government
HKND	Honk Kong Nicaragua Canal Development
IACHR	Inter-American Commission of Human Rights
ILO	International Labour Organization

INIDE	Instituto Nacional de Información de Desarrollo—National Institute of Development Information
MARENA	Ministerio del Medio Ambiente y Recursos Naturales—Ministry of the Environment and Natural Resources
MASTA	Miskitu Asla Takanka—Miskitu Indigenous People Unity
MRS	Movimiento Renovador Sandinista—Sandinista Renovation Movement (political party)
PLI	Partido Liberal Independiente—Independent Liberal Party
NGO	Non-Governmental Organization
PIDHDD	Plataforma Interamericana de Derechos Humanos, Democracia y Desarrollo—Inter-American Platform of Human Rights, Democracy and Development
RACCN	Región Autónoma de la Costa Caribe Norte—Autonomous Region of the North Caribbean Coast (previously RAAN Región Autónoma del Atlántico Norte —Autonomous Region of the North Atlantic)
RACCS	Región Autónoma de la Costa Caribe Sur—Autonomous Region of the South Caribbean Coast (previously RAAS Región Autónoma del Atlántico Sur—Autonomous Region of the South Atlantic)
UN	United Nations
UNDP	United Nations Development Programme
UNESCO	United Nations Educational, Scientific and Cultural Organization
URACCAN	Universidad de las Regiones Autónomas de la Costa Caribe de Nicaragua—University of the Autonomous Regions of the Caribbean Coast of Nicaragua
YATAMA	Yapti Tasba Masraka Nanih Aslatakanka—Children of Mother Earth (Miskito political party)
WOLA	Washington Office on Latin America
WTO	World Trade Organization

Glossary

Campesino	Small or subsistence farmer
Caudillismo	Strongman politics that is intolerant of dissent or opposition
Colono	Settler
Comandante	Military commander
Costeños	Inhabitants of the Caribbean Coast
Grupo de choque	Mob
Guardatinaja	Paca
Guatusa	Agouti
Manzana	A unit to measure land. One manzana is 7042m2 or 1.74 acres
Mestizo	Mixed race
Mestizaje	Racial mixing
Tercero	Third party

List of Figures

Chapter 1
Introduction: Democracy and Authoritarianism in Nicaragua

Abstract This chapter outlines contemporary threats to democracy in Nicaragua and introduces our analysis of the nation's growing authoritarianism, plans for the construction of a highly controversial interoceanic canal and aspects of the government's discursive and communications strategies. It draws on recent work produced under the banner of agnotology and considers attempts to produce public ignorance as dimensions of the Nicaraguan government's strategy for the evasion of criticism and the consolidation of power. We argue that such strategies must be understood in racialized and colonial terms that highlight historical relationships between Nicaragua's *mestizo* elites and its indigenous and Afro-descendant populations. In this context of expanding authoritarianism, many Nicaraguans are engaging in diverse forms of media activism that challenge and disrupt the government's struggles for hegemony.

Keywords Authoritarianism · Democracy · Media · Interoceanic canal Agnotology · Sandinista Front

If you travel through Reparto El Carmen, a middle-class suburb in Managua and the location of the mansion and presidential office of Nicaraguan president Daniel Ortega, you will find an exaggerated police presence. In the residential suburb that surrounds the five metre high, 370 metre long wall that protects the presidential building, there are twelve police checkpoints with at least two police officers stationed at each one to provide the president with round-the-clock protection (Almanza and Cruz 2013). Residents in this area live practically under siege. They require permission to enter, leave, move around their neighbourhood and receive visitors (Fig. 1.1). While the security far exceeds anything put in place by previous Nicaraguan presidents, it is perhaps clear why Ortega fears for his safety. Since his return to power in 2006, he and his wife Rosario Murillo have been busy developing and deploying a range of mechanisms that are dismantling Nicaragua's fragile democracy. They have taken effective control of all four branches of government as well as the army and police. They have been accused of deploying

J. Cupples and K. Glynn, *Shifting Nicaraguan Mediascapes*,
SpringerBriefs in Latin American Studies,
https://doi.org/10.1007/978-3-319-64319-9_1

Fig. 1.1 Map of Nicaragua showing location of key sites *Source* Marney Brosnan

fraudulent and highly irregular electoral practices (see Cupples 2009; McConnell 2014; Navas y Álvarez 2015). They have failed to uphold and implement laws passed by the National Assembly. They have contravened the Nicaraguan Constitution.[1] They have all but ceased to gather and publish data on development and environmental indicators. They frequently use violent mobs (*grupos de choque*) and riot police to intimidate opposition protestors and quash peaceful opposition

[1]Daniel Ortega's reelection in 2011 and 2016 violates Article 147 of the Nicaraguan Constitution.

protests. They have privatised foreign aid from Venezuela, effectively keeping it out of the national budget.[2] Over the course of 2015 and 2016, a series of conflicts between the Ortega government and the United Nations Development Program (UNDP) in Nicaragua led to the loss of US$60 million of development aid and the departure of nearly all office staff. These conflicts emerged as a result of the Nicaraguan government's attempts to prevent development aid from being channelled through NGOs, and its levelling of accusations against the UNDP for putatively distorting official data and 'meddling' in Nicaragua's political affairs (González N 2016a, 2016b). Ortega and Murillo have removed critical voices from the corridors of power and rewarded those who toe the party line.[3] They have bought, co-opted or silenced many independent media operations and have produced a climate of fear that makes it difficult for people to speak out. They have administered anti-poverty programmes in a highly clientelistic way so that only a small minority of party loyalists benefit from them. They have clamped down on women's rights, eliminated the right to therapeutic abortion, sent riot police to oversee and intimidate International Women's Day celebrants and temporarily detained feminist activists (see Kampwirth 2008; Jubb 2013; Romero 2016b).[4] According to Nina Lakhani (2015), the government has produced inaccurate official statistics on maternal mortality in an attempt to hide the consequences of its complete ban on abortion. Moreover, Nicaragua's poor score on Transparency International's Corruption Perceptions Index ranks it in 130th place out of 168 countries.[5] An increasingly authoritarian power-bloc has thus emerged, led by Daniel Ortega and Rosario Murillo in alliance with the Supreme Electoral Council, the Judiciary, most of the National Assembly, the security forces and much of the mainstream media that collectively work to ignore or suppress any event, process or claim that defies Orteguismo.

While it deploys anti-imperialist, socialist and Christian discourses, the power-bloc nevertheless works through mechanisms of corporate capitalism and the apparatuses of big business. Currently, the government is pursuing the construction of a $50 billion interoceanic canal backed by Chinese foreign investment. This highly neoliberal and

[2]Principally, $3,400 million received from Venezuela is not included in the national budget (Univisión Noticias 2015). The dramatic collapse of oil prices and death of Hugo Chávez have stemmed the flow of aid.

[3]Since returning to power in 2006, the FSLN has removed 33 elected mayors and vice mayors from power, stripped four National Assembly deputies of their seats and removed six territorial presidents elected by their communities in accordance with autonomy legislation. In all cases, either no reason or only highly suspect ones have been provided (García Peralta 2015; Redacción Central/Trinchera de la Noticia 2015; Villareal and Silva 2016).

[4]'Therapeutic abortion' refers to procedures arising from rape, incest, or risks associated with childbirth that endanger the life of the mother.

[5]According to Transparency International, the country's 'score indicates the perceived level of public sector corruption on a scale of 0 (highly corrupt) to 100 (very clean)'. (Nicaragua scores 27 on this scale.) Among all Latin America and Caribbean nations, only Haiti and Venezuela achieved poorer scores. Complete results for 2015 are available here: http:/www.transparency.org/cpi2015#results-table (see also Silva 2016).

colonial megaproject threatens to undermine Nicaragua's sovereignty, displace thousands of *campesinos* and indigenous and Afro-descendant peoples from their lands, and produce dramatic and irreversible environmental and biodiversity destruction. Yet the government declined to heed widespread calls for a peer-reviewed environmental impact assessment carried out by independent scientists (they instead commissioned a report by a commercial British consultancy; see Schneider 2015; Williams-Guillén 2015). The government also refused to conduct legally mandated consultation with affected communities (Centro Humboldt 2014; Huete-Pérez et al. 2015; Membreño 2016; Wade 2016). As Carlos Salinas (2015) writes, Daniel Ortega produces 'inflammatory discourse against imperialism, but took only 24 hours to hand a concession for the construction of the canal to [Chinese billionaire] Wang Jing'. Furthermore, this project 'has been negotiated in complete opacity by the authorities in Managua' (*La Jornada* 2015, our translation).

When the Environmental and Social Impact Assessment (ESIA) produced by British consulting firm ERM was eventually released to the public, it comprised 11,000 pages spread over 14 volumes available only in English. This is reminiscent of WTO panel reports on trade disputes that often consist of 20,000–40,000 pages filled with legalistic arcana that seems designed to prevent public engagement (Peet 2009: 216). Moreover, not only is ERM's ESIA written in a language not spoken by most Nicaraguans, but also it is accessible only through the Internet, to which many of the communities that will be directly affected by the canal, if it goes ahead, lack access. Yet, in its recommendations, ERM notes the lack of 'broad community support' in the 'Project-Affected Communities' and states that 'it is critical that sufficient time be allowed for the public to review this ESIA and understand the Project effects' (ERM 2015: np, Chap. 14, Sect. 14.1.1). Despite the practical impossibility of this recommendation, it is worth noting that the ERM report (which has been criticized by independent scientists for its inadequacies) expresses a high degree of caution about the project.[6] While it is not at all clear what ERM means by the phrase 'under normal situations' in the following extract (nor what, by implication, this language reveals about the actually existing current situation), they state that

> all routes for a Canal de Nicaragua through the Study Area would have significant environmental and social impacts, as essentially all of the economically feasible routes would

[6]As Circle of Blue's Keith Schneider (2015) reports, four chapters of the ESIA were submitted to a panel of independent scientists, who characterised its scientific conclusions as 'indefensible', 'implausible', 'wrong' and 'not realistic'. At present, as the panel report notes, Lake Nicaragua is not deep enough to accommodate large cargo ships and will require extensive dredging to increase its depth to almost 30 metres. The excavation project would also create 1.1 billion metric tonnes of silt that would need to be dumped outside of the dredging channel. It could potentially raise oxygen levels to the point where no fish could survive. It is not even certain, particularly in light of Nicaragua's growing drought susceptibility, that there is sufficient water supply to accommodate the two monumental locks that the project requires. ERM's ESIA is available on the HKND website at http://hknd-group.com/portal.php?mod=view&aid=293. The response from the independent panel is available here: http://www.circleofblue.org/waternews/wp-content/uploads/2015/06/Nicaragau-FIU-Panel-Summary.13-April-2015-Final.pdf.

> need to traverse internationally recognized protected areas, legally-recognized indigenous land, and Lago de Nicaragua, all of which under normal situations would be considered no-go areas. ERM considers the proposed route (i.e. Route 4) as the only route with the *potential* to adequately mitigate/offset its impacts and meet international standards. This determination was contingent on HKND providing funding and coordinating with the Government of Nicaragua to assure the restoration and permanent enforcement of the proposed Designated Preservation Area (…), in addition to other environmental and social mitigation and offset measures recommended in this ESIA. Absent these commitments, even Route 4 would not be able to achieve no net loss or meet international good practice (ERM 2015: np, Sect. 14.1.2).

It is not clear at the time of this writing whether the canal project will actually go ahead, and many people both within and beyond Nicaragua hope it will not.[7]

Contemporary Nicaragua is characterised by multiple forms of insecurity, persistent poverty and political tension. Nevertheless, government discourse embraces a triumphalist rhetoric of love, peace, prosperity, solidarity and happiness, and evades engagement with the nation's most deeply entrenched problems. This evasion is perhaps best symbolised by ubiquitous larger than life billboards bearing the face of Daniel Ortega (Fig. 1.2) and the so-called 'árboles de la vida' or 'trees of life' (Figs. 1.3 and 1.4) that line Managua's streets. The government has spent US $3.3 million to adorn Managua's main thoroughfares with 134 illuminated metallic trees (a figure that does not include the cost of burning 15,000 LED bulbs in each tree; see Moncada and Silva 2015). In April 2016, the Ortega government drew widespread criticism from Nicaraguan citizens and caused alarm among the neighbouring countries of Honduras and Costa Rica (see Romero 2016a) when it announced the purchase of 50 Russian armoured T7B1 tanks at a cost of $80 million, ostensibly to combat drug trafficking. To many, Ortega is starting to look a lot like the dictator Somoza he fought to overthrow in the 1970s. But the government's extreme levels of secrecy and repeated use of *grupos de choque* and riot police suggest perhaps that Daniel Ortega's hold on power is increasingly precarious. While Ortega has managed to maintain his leadership position through a combination of controversial changes to electoral law, diverse forms of clientelism and co-optation, and a measure of historic loyalty to the Revolution among sections of the electorate, popular consent to *Orteguista* sensemaking is becoming increasingly difficult to secure, and there is evidence that the cultural and political terrain of the nation is shifting.

This book was written during the year preceding the 2016 presidential elections, which gave Daniel Ortega a third consecutive term in office, but lacked both credibility and legitimacy, and were characterized by high levels of abstention (Cerda and Miranda 2016). At the time of writing, there are two main groups that threaten Daniel's grip on power. The first consists of well-educated,

---

[7]In January 2015, China and Latin America held their first ever ministerial level meeting, the China-CELAC forum, in Beijing. The meeting aimed to strengthen economic cooperation between the two regions, and was attended by four presidents and 20 foreign ministers. It is worth noting, as MRS deputy Enrique Sáenz (2016) points out, that there was no representation from Nicaragua, nor was the canal project even mentioned.

Fig. 1.2 Billboard of Daniel Ortega Source: Photo by author

Fig. 1.3 The 'trees of life' Source: Photo by author

Fig. 1.4 The 'trees of life' Source: Photo by author

Managua-based Sandinista dissidents who fought in the Revolution but have since left or been expelled from the FSLN. Some are now part of a breakaway party known as the Sandinista Renovation Movement (MRS), many work in development or feminist NGOs and most are active on social media. The second group is the indigenous and Afro-descendant populations, collectively referred to as Costeños, who inhabit the Caribbean Coast and have a long history of conflict with both Managua-based governments in general and the FSLN in particular. They have been fighting for historical restitution and rights, and are feeling increasingly frustrated by the political obstacles that stand in the way of regional autonomy and legal recognition of ownership of their lands. These two groups occupy very different political geographies within Nicaragua and have generally distinct political concerns that converge in their shared opposition to Sandinista authoritarianism, corruption and perpetration of electoral fraud, and in their mutual resistance to the canal project. It is crucial to recognize that the sharp differences between Pacific and Caribbean activists and cultures more broadly stem from the distinct colonial and postcolonial histories of these two regions. While Sandinista authoritarianism shapes political engagement throughout the country, the people of Caribbean Nicaragua (which includes parts of the transnational region known as the Mosquito Coast or *la Moskitia*) must generally negotiate a variety of forms of coloniality, racism and Othering. As Costeño writer and filmmaker, Larry Montenegro Baena (2017) wrote in a public Facebook status posted in March 2017,

> Let's not get confused. One thing is to fight for socio-historical rights from a region historically excluded by the State (Moskitia), another is to fight from a region that has been historically privileged (Pacific) against a dictatorship. It will never be the same [struggle]. In the Moskitia, we are not fighting against a dictatorship, but rather against a colonial regime that has imposed dictatorships of all kinds in detriment of its self-determination as a region. In this sense, in the Moskitia we have been fighting for more than a century, since we became part of the [Nicaraguan] State. So without minimising the struggle taking place in the Pacific, our struggle from here is deeper, as is this historic wound that won't heal with a change of government.[8]

Ortega's strategy is not only an authoritarian one but also a decisively colonial one that seeks to produce and deploy forms of ignorance to produce and sustain hegemony. In this book, we draw on recent work from the emergent field of agnotology, which aims to bring critical theoretical resources and perspectives to bear on the strategic production of ignorance in a variety of different contexts. Efforts to produce or promote ignorance can operate through a range of mechanisms and techniques that include even such practices as 'deliberate or inadvertent neglect, secrecy and suppression, document destruction, unquestioned tradition and myriad forms of inherent (or unavoidable) culturopolitical selectivity' (Proctor and Schiebinger 2008: vii). As Tom Slater (2012: 951) writes, it is important to 'consider ignorance as a *strategic and pernicious ploy,* an active construct' that ruling groups will use if they can to produce and maintain their hegemony. The power relations associated with coloniality impart a particular cast to strategies for the production of ignorance, for coloniality always involves at its core a set of imperializing epistemological practices. As Walter Mignolo (2005) reminds us, one of the main consequences of coloniality in 'Latin' America has been the mobilization of the discourses of Eurocentric modernity and modernization to suppress, marginalize, invalidate, erase and demonise black and indigenous knowledges and identities. In this sense, we view the production of ignorance, in Foucauldian fashion, as part of the broader practices and processes through which knowledge is produced and deployed as an agent of power and control. Boaventura de Sousa Santos (2004: 238) promotes a 'sociology of absences' whose function is somewhat similar to that of agnotology, in that it serves to reveal the ways in which hegemonic social formations seek to 'destroy non-hegemonic and potentially counter-hegemonic social experience'. Thus, the sociology of absences 'consists of an inquiry that aims to explain that what does not exist is, in fact, actively produced as non-existent, that is, as a non-credible alternative to what exists. The objective of the sociology of absences is to transform impossible into possible objects, absent into present objects'.

Indeed, Eurocentrism itself is supported by a sustained 'will-to-ignorance' that is built upon 'patterns of silencing' that 'articulate with, and accommodate… formulas of knowledge production, consolidation and consumption that trivialise existing power arrangements and enduring political struggles' (Rodríguez Maeso and

[8]Available at https://www.facebook.com/larry.montenegrobaena?fref=ts&ref=br_tf# (our translation).

Araújo 2015: 4). For Noel Cazenave (2015), those who benefit from racialized forms of oppression suffer from a syndrome he labels 'IPA', which refers to 'the *ignorance* of not knowing, the *privilege* of not needing to know, and the *arrogance* of not wanting to know' (emphasis added). Moreover, in the contemporary era, official discourses of multiculturalism, oriented around the endorsement and celebration of ethnic diversity by the Latin American political class, become 'the concealing mechanism par excellence for new forms of colonization' (Rivera Cusicanqui 2012: 99). Official multiculturalism, as Juliet Hooker (2005a) has demonstrated, is a useful way for *mestizo* states to increase their legitimacy, while neutralising the more radical cultural politics of racialized groups. Although the growing authoritarianism of Ortega's government has been widely recognized (see *inter alia* Carroll 2008; Feinberg 2011; Smith 2011; Leyden-Sussler 2014), the Nicaraguan power-bloc's strategies of hegemonization have racialized dimensions that have not been adequately analysed.

While we argue that the situation is undoubtedly troubling, an analysis of the media activism of contemporary social movements in a rapidly changing mediasphere suggests it is a highly fluid one. Given the conflicting forces at work within contemporary social formations in Nicaragua and the commitment we share with our research participants to decolonizing modes of political transformation, we have deployed conjunctural analysis of discursive struggles as our primary methodological technique. As Stuart Hall and his colleagues argue, the Gramscian/Althusserian concept of the 'conjuncture' refers to 'a specific moment in the life of a social formation… when the antagonisms and contradictions, which are always at work in society, begin to '"*fuse*" into a *ruptural unity*' [Althusser 1969: 99]… which may result in a more general social crisis' (Hall et al. 2013: xv, emphasis in original). Our work draws on in-depth fieldwork in Nicaragua, conducted over many years, and most recently involving indigenous and Afro-descendant broadcasters, media makers and users, and other activists located on the Caribbean Coast. It is based primarily on interviews and participant observation conducted in Bilwi (Puerto Cabezas), Bluefields and Pearl Lagoon between 2007 and 2016, along with analysis of a range of media texts from community and mainstream television, radio, newspapers and social media sites such as Facebook and YouTube. We believe that key features of the current conjuncture involving the mobilization and mediation of social movements have important implications for the stability of hegemonic control. This book explores these dynamics through diverse forms of mediated activism taking place in an increasingly authoritarian Nicaragua.

Our research is part of a broader project that is focused on the geographies of media convergence. We are exploring the cultural and political potentials emerging in the new media environment for struggles over black and indigenous identities, rights and modes of cultural citizenship. With conceptual tools drawn from decolonial and other contemporary cultural theories, we explore and analyse uses of media by both black and indigenous groups on the Caribbean Coast and by oppositional social movements in the Pacific region of Nicaragua, sites marked by growing authoritarianism, de-democratisation and in the case of the Caribbean, entrenched coloniality. The next chapter situates Nicaraguan current events within a broader Latin American context and in relation to changes in the new media environment. We suggest that in order to grasp the potential for political transformation in this context, we need to consider the changes in the nature of social movements in Latin America after decades of neoliberalism and a shift to left-wing authoritarian populism, in conjunction with phenomena often associated with digitalization and media convergence that is giving rise to new media geographies. In Chap. 3, we outline the current conjuncture in Nicaragua, with a focus on dimensions that are most pertinent to our analysis. In particular, we describe the struggles for Caribbean Coast autonomy and changes in the Nicaraguan mediascape that involve both official and grassroots media. Chapter 4 deals with mediated responses to the current crisis on the Caribbean Coast and setbacks to regional struggles for land rights. Chapter 5 moves to the Pacific region and provides several examples of ways that Sandinista control over the mediascape is disrupted by interventions and content sharing by ordinary citizens. The final chapter returns to questions of the production of ignorance and illegibility by looking at how current Sandinista strategies generate gaps and absences that invite decolonial and democratising media interventions. While this book focuses on contemporary cultural politics in Nicaragua, the material we examine has pertinence beyond the Nicaraguan context for understanding contemporary strategies for the production of ignorance, as well as the implications of emergent mediascapes for struggles to promote cultural citizenship, democracy, and indigenous and Afro-descendant rights. We aim as well to contribute to the theorization of media convergence and digitalization in relation to the global South.

Chapter 2
Decolonial Social Movements, Leftist Governments and the Media

Abstract This chapter situates events in Nicaragua within a broader Latin American context and in relation to changes that have been actively producing a new media environment in the region. We consider both changes in the nature of social movements in Latin America after decades of neoliberalism and a shift to left-wing authoritarian populism, and the emergence of new media geographies associated with digitalization and media convergence. We show that the contemporary Latin American media environment is a highly contradictory, paradoxical and multidiscursive one in which a plurality of voices can find and forge new forms and spaces of expression.

Keywords Social movements · Media convergence · Clientelism
Decoloniality · Resistance · Indigenous peoples · Afro-descended peoples

The myriad failures of neoliberalism across Latin America have in recent decades led to substantial social movement mobilization and the election of a number of governments touting explicitly anti-neoliberal platforms. Under these so-called pink tide governments, there have been attempts to reduce poverty and nationalise natural resource extraction in order to channel profits towards social programmes. In many Latin American countries, during the same period, the struggles for indigenous and to a lesser extent Afro-descendant rights have gained new forms of political momentum and visibility. As a result, the concept of plurinationality has also found its way into a number of Latin American constitutions and the official appropriation of the indigenous concept of *buen vivir* in Bolivia and Ecuador has dislodged the political authority of neoliberal capitalism. These cultural and political shifts, while important, cannot be seen as bringing an end to neoliberalism or coloniality, and it is important to recognize that Latin America's leftist governments are not as progressive nor as democratic as might appear to outsiders. As Raúl Madrid et al. (2010: 146) write, 'in an effort to strengthen their hold on power, they have re-written the constitution to allow for their own re-election, dissolved or manipulated the legislature and stacked traditional nonpartisan institutions with their supporters'. In most countries, there are important continuities with the neoliberal model as economies continue to be based on predatory forms of capital

J. Cupples and K. Glynn, *Shifting Nicaraguan Mediascapes*,
SpringerBriefs in Latin American Studies,
https://doi.org/10.1007/978-3-319-64319-9_2

accumulation or resource extraction. As Raúl Zibechi (2012) acknowledges, the poverty reduction programmes in a number of Latin American countries reduce poverty without substantially redistributing wealth.

Daniel Ortega's use of clientelistic mechanisms such as Zero Poverty programmes and the top-down creation of Councils of Citizen Power (CPCs) replicates models used in pink tide countries, most notably Venezuela. Ortega's strategy is therefore not unique, but it is important to note that unlike the election of Rafael Correa in Ecuador or Evo Morales in Bolivia, Ortega was returned to power not through social movement mobilization, but rather through the formation of problematic pacts between the ruling Liberals and the Sandinista-controlled Supreme Electoral Council to change the electoral law (Cupples and Larios 2005).[1] During its long period in opposition, the FSLN failed to rebuild a base of popular support that included younger Nicaraguans who did not experience the revolution or the civil war of the 1980s. Furthermore, they managed to alienate or expel from the party many of those who had. Hence there are many prominent, well-respected and outspoken revolutionary Nicaraguans who have distanced themselves from the FSLN and are openly critical of Ortega's actions. They are former guerrilla fighters and commanders, government ministers, and intellectuals, artists and writers who are historically recognized for their decisive contributions to the toppling of Somoza and the project of revolutionary transformation. They include Sergio Ramírez, Gioconda Belli, Dora María Téllez, Henry Ruiz, Hugo Torres, Victor Tirado López, Luis Carrión, Ernesto Cardenal, Mónica Baltodano, Victor Hugo Tinoco, René Vivas, Luis Enrique Mejía Godoy, Daisy Zamora and Vidaluz Meneses. These are the prominent names those who are, along with Daniel Ortega and Tomás Borge, central to any history of the Nicaraguan Revolution.

Shortly after they regained power in 2006, the FSLN tried to use the CPCs to replace the existing grassroots civil society organizations that had been mobilising against neoliberal policies for the previous decade and a half, though this FSLN strategy met with only limited success. Nevertheless, some grassroots activists did start working or collaborating with the Sandinista government, for which they often received paid positions, scholarships for their children or other goods in return for their political support. The FSLN's clientelistic strategies make little sense from a community development perspective, but appear more effective as a means to secure and maintain electoral support and political control for the ruling party. For example, the political secretary of the Sandinista Front in the Creole community of Pearl Lagoon in the South Caribbean told us that the government was providing 25 families with two years of government-funded satellite television from multinational Mexican-based telecommunications corporation Claro. When we asked how they identified the families whose satellite TV bills would be paid for by the government, he said it went to people who belong to the 'poorest class' and whose

[1]Daniel Ortega, now in his 70s, has been the leader of the FSLN without interruption since the triumph of the Revolution in 1979. He won the elections of 1984 and the last three in 2006, 2011 and 2016. He lost in 1990, 1996 and 2001.

homes and way of living are 'not quite good'. We've been told repeatedly by ordinary Nicaraguans that the bestowal of such largess upon some poor families functions principally as a form of electoral bribery to increase and maintain popular support for the FSLN. These accounts suggest, at the very least, the existence of widespread popular scepticism towards the government and its policies and objectives. Such scepticism is readily understandable in light of the fact that, despite an average economic growth rate of 3.6%, large amounts of Venezuelan aid, selective handouts for supporters and the implementation of so-called zero poverty programmes, living conditions in Nicaragua have barely improved in the decade since the FSLN regained power. According to figures from the Nicaraguan Central Bank (BCN), purchasing power for formal sector employees in 2015 was almost ten percent lower than it was in 2006 (Alvarez Hidalgo 2016).[2]

With respect to the impacts of pink tide governments on social movements, Zibechi (2012) notes two main tendencies, one negative and another more positive. He demonstrates how the post-neoliberal turn, through which social activists put progressive governments into power, has tended to neutralise the counter-hegemonic effects of social movements, which has led in some cases to their fragmentation and demobilization. For example, in Ecuador, government cooptation seriously weakened the mobilizational capacity and political influence of the Confederation of Indigenous Nationalities of Ecuador (CONAIE), which was previously one of the most vibrant and active indigenous movements in all of Latin America. Zibechi views the enrolment of previously marginalized populations in state-led social movements and anti-poverty programmes as mechanisms designed to control and domesticate the movements in particular and the broader population in general. Consequently, however, the modalities and spatialities of power deployed by social movements are beginning to shift in important ways. As Zibechi (2012: 269) writes, there are large sections of societies 'that are now uncontrollable and impossible to discipline through repression'. Hence the top-down, vertical and molar forms of power exerted by state agents are increasingly outmaneuvered by horizontal, spontaneous, immanent, dispersed and molecular forms of power and evasion mobilized by social movements like the recovered factories movement in Argentina, which has deployed stealth, opportunism, non-hierarchical practices and alternative exchange relations as a means of implementing non-capitalist modes and zones of production. Zibechi's (2010) account of everyday life and political organisation in El Alto, Bolivia, where there is no practical distinction between ends and means, demonstrates how it is possible to reproduce non-capitalist economies and keep the state at a distance. Under such conditions, the power-bloc must attempt to 'domesticate' or 'redirect' the social movements 'so that they benefit the ruling class', but the 'organizational dispersion' of these movements is proving 'far more potent than the centralized state' and enabling social groups to create and defend their own autonomous spaces (Zibechi 2010: 309). The tactical

[2]According to Alvarez Hidalgo (2016), a formal sector worker earned an average of 4,823.9 córdobas in 2006. By August 2015, average monthly wages had fallen to 4,358.4 córdobas.

responses of these social movements to dominating powers are underpinned and motivated by popular, black, indigenous and decolonial ways of knowing and being. They both contribute to and draw upon the growing epistemological crisis that afflicts Eurocentric rationality, as a political contestation of both extreme wealth inequalities and capitalist-driven climate change motivates and facilitates the assertion and circulation of alternative and historically repressed pluriversal knowledges (Quijano 2007; Escobar 2010). What de Sousa Santos (2014) calls the epistemologies of the south are responding to the intensifying failure of Eurocentric modernity to attend to the problems it has created. We need therefore to recognize that 'the emancipatory transformations in the world may follow grammars and scripts other than those developed by Western-centric critical theory' (de Sousa Santos 2014: viii).

It is an error to assume that there are singular Latin American societies comprised of disadvantaged groups that appeal to the state for redress (Zibechi 2012). Rather there are two asymmetrically opposed societies, 'an official society, hegemonic and of colonial heritage' (Zibechi 2012: 318), and another that is based on an indigenous cosmovision, indigenous modes of governance and justice, and non-capitalist community relations in which 'the past—not a modernist future—inspires action' (Zibechi 2012: 328). In his interrogation of the 'Latin' in Latin America, Walter Mignolo (2005: xv) notes that indigenous and Afro-descendant peoples across the continent are 'unfolding new knowledge projects that are making the idea of Latin America obsolete', so *mestizo* Latin America must co-exist with these social and cultural alternatives that do not disappear, despite historical and contemporary assimilation policies and the persistence of racialized democracies and discursive formations (see Wade 1997; Cupples 2013). In Nicaragua, the interactions between these competing social formations and modalities of power is producing a conjunctural crisis in the vertical, *mestizo* and Eurocentric state, which increasingly fails to achieve hegemony by popular consent and must therefore resort to strategies for the production of ignorance (which we might regard as a *politics of not knowing*), along with ever more coercive forms of control, including the rampant application of state-led repression and violence.

The important changes in the temporalities, spatialities and tactical maneuvers of social movements are both enabled and paralleled by contemporary transformations in the media environment. Centralised media systems are increasingly disrupted and decentered through their interactions with new media platforms and mobilities. On the one hand, the contemporary media environment involves intensifying concentrations of media ownership and practices of conglomeration linked with mergers, acquisitions and the synergistic expansion of vertical and horizontal integration. Moreover, there are ongoing and alarming expansions and accelerations of both governmental and corporate forms and practices of mediated surveillance, tracking and algorithmic control. On the other hand, these processes are developing in tandem with a democratisation of media access that is enabling ordinary citizens to both produce their own media, and respond to and interact with content generated by conglomerates and official channels in ways that can sometimes be politically transformative (see, for example, Jenkins 2006; Martín-Barbero 2011; Jenkins et al.

2013; Cupples and Glynn 2013, 2014b, 2016; Castells 2012; Juris 2008). As Jesús Martín-Barbero (2011: 42) observes, new media forms and technologies 'are increasingly being appropriated by groups from lowly sectors, making *socio-cultural revenge* or a form of *socio-cultural return match* possible for them, that is, the construction of a counter-hegemony all over the world'. It is apparent that 'old' as well as 'new' media, and 'mainstream', 'community' and 'indigenous' media all provide resources for the construction of cultural citizenship among subordinated populations.[3] While members of both the dominant and subordinated sectors recognize that the media, broadly speaking, constitute powerful forces for or against political and social transformation, the contemporary mediascapes constitute a complex and dynamic articulation of modes of production and reception, texts, discourses, narratives and images that increasingly escapes the direct control of any particular social class or formation.

The contemporary media environment is then a highly contradictory one, fraught with surveillance and countersurveillance, consumerism and opposition, control and resistance. It is one in which a plurality of voices can find spaces of articulation, and dominant discourses are routinely rearticulated as they traverse increasingly interlinked media networks and platforms. The demands of marginalized and subordinated populations for human rights and cultural citizenship are increasingly forged through grassroots media practices and within what Manuel Castells (2007: 246) calls 'horizontal networks of interactive communication'. These networks have enabled social movements to '[escape] their confinement in the fragmented space of places and [seize] the global space of flows, while not virtualizing themselves to death, keeping their local experience and the landing sites of their struggle as the material foundation of their ultimate goal: the restoration of meaning in the new space/time of our existence, made of both flows, places and their interaction' (Castells 2007: 257). New tactical media uses and mobilities facilitate forms of countersurveillance and sometimes provide a measure of protection and maneuverability for subordinated peoples.[4] Counterhegemonic discourses and struggles articulate with one another as they cross the networked mediasphere in ways that enhance their visibility and political effectivity. Indigenous and Afro-descended communities around the world have been producing their own media in order to participate in horizontal networks with states, civil society organizations and other indigenous groups, to contest colonial relations of power, to produce counter-representations, to circulate counter-histories, to promote cultural and linguistic revitalization and to engage more effectively in activism aimed at the

[3] We use scare quotes here to emphasise the instability and contingency of these media formations and categories, as well as the ways in which they converge and overlap within the contemporary mediascape.

[4] We recognize that visibility in the media also puts activists' lives at risk and that Central America continues to be a dangerous place for political activism, as demonstrated by the 2016 murders of environmental activists Berta Cáceres and Nelson García in Honduras, and the 2009 assassination of Salvadoran environmental activist Marcelo Rivera.

attainment of autonomy and land rights.[5] At the same time, digitally connected citizens use computers and smartphones to speak back to mainstream media corporations, and to remix and share content that circulates and resonates with alternative sensemaking strategies or political and cultural ambitions. The next chapter examines these two key elements of the contemporary conjuncture: changes in indigenous and Afro-descendant social movements, and transformations of the Nicaraguan mediascape.

[5]There is a large and growing literature on indigenous media. See, *inter alia*, Weatherford 1990; Ginsburg 1991; Turner 1992; Glynn and Tyson 2007; Himpele 2008; Wilson and Stewart 2008; Schiwy 2009; Wilson 2015. On indigenous media on the Caribbean Coast of Nicaragua, see Glynn and Cupples 2011 and Cupples and Glynn 2014a, 2014b.

Chapter 3
Constructing the Nicaraguan Conjuncture

Abstract This chapter outlines the current conjuncture in Nicaragua and focuses in particular on struggles for Caribbean Coast autonomy in the face of growing *mestizo* hostility and intensified migratory pressures within the region. It also outlines key changes within both official Nicaraguan and grassroots media. While the government has undertaken serious efforts to undermine the freedom and independence of media in Nicaragua, citizens and activists are developing and deploying innovative media tactics of their own.

Keywords Autonomy · Migration · Mestizaje · Racism · Law
Press freedom

3.1 Caribbean Coast Autonomy

While the early years of the Sandinista Revolution are remembered by many Nicaraguans and international supporters as a period of liberation and revolutionary transformation, the experience of many of Nicaragua's indigenous (Miskito, Mayangna and Rama) and Creole (Afro-descended) peoples who live mostly in two autonomous regions on the Caribbean Coast was quite different. While there were important political alliances and shared goals between Miskito, Creole and Pacific *mestizo* political actors in the 1980s, these alliances very quickly began to unravel with tragic consequences. Early in 1982 during the Contra War, in an operation that has come to be known as Red Christmas (Navidad Roja), Sandinista soldiers forcibly relocated 42 Miskito communities that were living close to the highly militarized Honduran border and destroyed their homes and crops. Many Miskitos were executed or died during the relocation. It was a cruel and highly insensitive move that, along with other factors, led many Miskitos to turn against the revolution and join the counter-revolutionary forces. Others became refugees and fled to the US, Honduras, or Costa Rica. The growing tensions between Sandinistas and indigenous peoples highlighted not only political differences but also cultural ones, and demonstrated how little understanding Pacific *mestizo* Nicaraguans had of the

J. Cupples and K. Glynn, *Shifting Nicaraguan Mediascapes*,
SpringerBriefs in Latin American Studies,
https://doi.org/10.1007/978-3-319-64319-9_3

worldviews and cultural practices of the Caribbean Coast (see Nietschmann 1989). As Galio Gurdián and Maricela Kauffmann (2002: 34–5, our translation) write:

> For the indigenous peoples and ethnic communities of the Caribbean Coast, the revolution and the revolutionaries constituted the epitome of *mestizo* ethnocentrism. For the revolution and its cadres, who were ignorant of the history of contradictions between the *mestizo* society on the Pacific and the Caribbean peoples, the Coast and its inhabitants had been rescued by the revolution and the ingenuous and arrogant slogan of the "awakening giant" (*el gigante que despierta*) showed that these people who were both backward and asleep were finally being redeemed.

Relations between the Pacific and the Caribbean parts of the country are then characterised by different forms of internal colonialism that include institutionalized and everyday racisms, social, economic and infrastructural neglect, environmental destruction, cultural imperialism, paternalism, and folkloricization. Even the government's unreliable statistics on poverty reduction (INIDE 2015, see note 14) place Caribbean Coast poverty at twice that of the Pacific region, while in the rural communities of the region it is estimated that poverty afflicts 70 percent of the population (Silva 2015; see also Cunningham Kain 2006). Poverty persists in spite of an average national economic growth rate of 4.9% for the last four years (Navas 2015a).

In addition to the environmental destruction wrought by the overexploitation of the region's marine, timber and mineral resources, Costeño lives, livelihoods, and cultures have been threatened for the past two decades by intense migratory pressures from the Pacific, which Costeños call the 'Pacific invasion'. *Mestizo* farmers from the Pacific region, referred to as *colonos* (settlers) or *terceros* (third parties), have settled on communal lands and are engaged in various modes of agricultural subsistence, cattle ranching and logging, resulting in substantial conflict and serious resource destruction. Their presence makes it impossible for the legal owners of the land to exercise their constitutional rights (Antonio 2008).

The process of internal colonialism began much earlier than the current Pacific invasion, however, as did the Costeño opposition to *mestizo* imperialisation. The region had never succumbed to Spanish rule and functioned for much of Nicaragua's colonial period as a British protectorate. In 1894, it was violently annexed by the Nicaraguan state, which gave rise to a long-term Costeño struggle for self-determination and cultural survival against a largely hostile *mestizo* society. In Nicaragua as elsewhere in Latin America, the ideology of *mestizaje*, or European and indigenous racial mixing, has created the conditions for the emergence of a widespread 'endophobia' across the continent: an anxious fear that indigenous and especially black identities and cultural communities constitute obstacles to development and nation-building (Duncan 2012; see also Hooker 2005b).[1] In Pacific

---

[1]Hooker (2005b) has charted the historical shifts and continuities in official *mestizo* nationalisms in Nicaragua, focusing on three key variants: the *vanguardismo* of the 1930s, *Sandinismo* of the 1960s, and *mestizo* multiculturalism of the 1990s. While these three types show key continuities, there are also significant differences in emphasis, particularly with respect to understanding the nature of the encounter between Europeans and indigenous peoples. What her work reveals is that

Nicaragua, the myth of *mestizaje* and concomitant endophobia are linked with the development of hegemonic and homogenizing ideologies of nationalism that have largely invisibilised the region's indigenous identities, practices and important political struggles (Gould 1998). Nevertheless, while the myth of *mestizaje* has had devastating consequences for indigenous communities located in Nicaragua's Pacific region, there have also been notable forms of indigenous cultural revitalization in the Pacific since the Sandinistas' first electoral defeat in 1990 (Gould 1998; also see Field 1999).

The forms of cultural erasure enacted by the myth of *mestizaje* are more extreme in relation to black identities than indigenous ones. In his book, *Tambor Olvidado*, Nicaraguan author Sergio Ramírez writes that dominant understandings of racial mixing (*mestizaje*) in Nicaragua are partial and exclusionary, as they recognize the encounter between native people and Europeans, but erase encounters with Africans. In spite of the fact that Nicaragua is a country that emerges from this triple hybridization and therefore has an undeniable African heritage, Ramírez (2007: 9) claims that 'we don't talk about that' ('*de eso no se habla*'). During the colonial era, slaves and other people of African descent could be found in both the Pacific and Caribbean parts of Nicaragua. However, most Nicaraguans today act as if African heritages have ceased to have any impact on the nation's contemporary identities, and whatever recognition there remains of Nicaragua's Africanness is now concentrated on the Caribbean Coast among the Black Creole population. For Ramírez, the dominant attitude gives rise to an historical amnesia and non-admission of the 'Africa that we carry within'. While *mestizaje* celebrates hybridity to a degree, it functions structurally and ideologically in Nicaragua in the way that whiteness does in the United States and Northern Europe. A comment from an *El Nuevo Diario* reader in response to an article about the Caribbean Coast (Aguirre 2015, our translation) characterises Britain's presence in the region prior to the twentieth century as an 'invasion' (whereas Costeños tend to regard it as a reciprocal trading relationship), and captures the mix of racism, ignorance and paternalism one often encounters from Pacific *mestizo* Nicaraguans:

> I think that that territory is Nicaraguan, full stop. The British occupation was an invasion but the territory can't be divided. Just as in the centre of the country there are indigenous communities, [but] that doesn't mean it is not Nicaraguan territory. The fact that the little black people (*los negritos*) have English surnames makes me think that they were brought here as slaves, just like in the US, and for them it was better that the English left, because now they are free, and now they are our little black people (*nuestros negritos*), and the government needs to treat them like all nationals and develop the region bit by bit.

In January 2014, *La Prensa* reported on how the *mestizo* manager of a Bluefields gas station that was running a competition had thrown out the coupons submitted by black taxi drivers, stating 'that while I am here, no black person is going to win a prize' (León C 2014). Everyday racisms are prevalent on the Caribbean Coast as well as in the Pacific region. Many Costeños have expressed concerns to us about

---

mestizo nationalism is extremely resilient and obstructs full citizenship for black and indigenous Costeños, but that it is also amenable to change.

the growing presence of *mestizo* culture and the Spanish language on the Coast, and the threat they pose to cultural practices, a phenomenon William Grigsby (2005) has called *españolización* or *mestizización*.

As a result of the long British presence in the region, both the Miskito and Creole people developed what Charles Hale (1992) calls an Anglo affinity: an appreciation for all things English. While British intervention in the region between the 17th and 19th centuries was certainly not benign, it was valued by the Miskitos, in part because it facilitated trade in key goods, but mainly because it kept the Spaniards out (Helms 1971; Hale 1992; Dennis 2004; Pineda 2006). In the 20th century, many US banana and lumber companies established themselves on the Coast and employed the English-speaking Creole population as managers, which further entrenched affinities for Anglophone cultural goods (including a love for baseball, US magazines and other consumer items brought on ships from New Orleans). Spanish-speaking *mestizos* view this Anglo affinity as deeply suspect. As Baron Pineda (2006: 3) writes,

> from the standpoint of Pacific Nicaraguan nationalism, the historical connection that the Mosquito Coast has had with Great Britain and the English-speaking world provokes suspicion and serves to place Costeño society as a suspect internal other. Throughout the Contra War the opposition of Costeños was viewed as a problem of separatism that was the residue of the hyper-exploitation of the region by British and North American colonialism and neo-colonialism.

Indeed, in the early years of the Sandinista revolution, black Costeños were either ignored or treated 'as potentially divisive agents of imperial foreign powers such as Britain and the United States' (Hooker 2005b: 27).

Costeño resistance to internal colonialism, in conjunction with the emergence of an international political climate that has become far more favourable to post-colonial redress for indigenous peoples (see Brysk 2000), means that a number of legislative and political spaces have been opened up for the pursuit of political rights by Nicaragua's indigenous and Afro-descendant peoples. The tragedy of Red Christmas and the political and military struggles that preceded and followed it culminated in the passage of an ambitious Autonomy Law (Law 28) in 1987, which created two new autonomous regions: the Autonomous Region of the North Atlantic (RAAN) and the Autonomous Region of the South Atlantic (RAAS).[2] The rights of indigenous and Afro-descended Nicaraguans to autonomy were also

[2]The two regions are now called the *Región Autónoma de la Costa Caribe Norte*/Autonomous Region of the North Caribbean Coast (RACCN), and the *Región Autónoma de la Costa Caribe Sur*/Autonomous Region of the South Caribbean Coast (RACCS). After the passage of the autonomy law, they were named *Región Autónoma del Atlántico Norte*/Autonomous Region of the North Atlantic (RAAN) and *Región Autónoma del Atlántico Sur*/Autonomous Region of the South Atlantic (RAAS). During the Somoza dictatorship, the two regions were collectively referred to as Zelaya. During the colonial era, the region was referred to as La Mosquitia. Today, as a result of frequent name changes, Costeños refer to their region as the Atlantic Coast, the Caribbean Coast and La Mosquitia, in addition to using the terms RAAN and RAAS. The term Zelaya is still used, but much less frequently.

recognized in the 1987 Nicaraguan Constitution, making the country one of the first in Latin America to grant collective legal rights to black and indigenous inhabitants (Hooker 2005b). It took 16 years of further struggle by Costeño communities, however, before the National Assembly would issue an essential legislative decree to regulate the terms of Law 28 by specifying the roles to be played by the autonomous regional governments and the ways for citizens to pursue their historic communal rights as indigenous and Afro-descendant peoples. This necessary step towards implementation of the 1987 autonomy law came as a direct result of an historic 2001 legal case in which the Inter-American Court of Human Rights ruled against the Nicaraguan state and upheld the Mayangna community of Awas Tingni's right to communal property, thus rescinding a highly damaging logging concession (see Grossman 2001; Hale 2005).

In 2003, the National Assembly also passed Law 445, known as the Law of the Communal Property Regime of the Indigenous Peoples and Ethnic Communities of the Autonomous Regions of the Atlantic Coast of Nicaragua and of the Rivers Bocay, Coco, Indio and Maíz, which codified natural resource management and communal property establishment procedures, and specifically addresses the presence of so-called *terceros* or *colonos* (*mestizo* settlers) on Costeño land. It is important to note that the FSLN, in opposition at the time, voted in favour of Law 445, but as Jennifer Goett (2006) observes, World Bank financial and political support rooted in a discourse of 'multicultural citizenship' (Hooker 2005a, 2005b) was crucial in securing its passage (see also Gordon et al. 2003). In order to facilitate the implementation of Law 445, the Miskito political party YATAMA formed an unlikely alliance with the FSLN to fight the 2006 presidential elections (Finley-Brook 2011). Their alliance would quickly break down as well-established hostilities reemerged and the FSLN, once returned to power, began to disrupt rather than support the autonomy process. Nevertheless, after the return of the FSLN to power in 2006, Nicaragua also supported global initiatives for indigenous rights by voting in favour of the UN Declaration of Indigenous Rights in 2007 and ratifying ILO Convention 169 in 2010.

Law 445 stipulates a five-stage process that was supposed to have been completed by 2010 (Antonio 2008). The process has been frustratingly slow, in part because of a lack of central government support, the distorting interventions of Pacific political parties, the legal inexperience of Costeño leaders, the fragmentation that exists within Miskito and Creole movements, and the disjuncture between Eurocentric modes of governance and jurisprudence and indigenous ones. Decades of discrimination meant that many Costeños lacked understanding of their own histories and did not see themselves as rights-bearing citizens of Nicaragua. Law 445's first four stages consist of the submission of applications, the settlement of disputes, and the measurement, demarcation and titling of lands. In 22 out of 23 communities, these four stages have now been completed. The final stage consists of title clearance or *saneamiento*, and relates specifically to the presence of third parties or *terceros*, who continue to reside illegally on titled communal lands. It is therefore crucial for both peace and the much-needed economic advancement of the Coast that Law 445 be fully implemented.

The FSLN has worked to secure political support on the Coast mainly through the recruitment and co-optation of local Costeño leaders. It is important to recognize that strategies to secure Sandinista hegemony are often delegated to Costeños, a move that is highly controversial and widely criticized, and that functions to divide ethnic communities (and is possibly intended to do so). As we shall argue, this approach also carries substantial political risks for Costeño politicians. Officially, the Sandinista government in Managua supports the establishment of Caribbean Coast autonomy, which it calls 'an historic project to which the Government of Reconciliation and National Unity is deeply committed' (Mairena 2014: 7, our translation). They even renamed 'Columbus Day' as the 'Day of Indigenous, Black and Popular Resistance', in honour of indigenous peoples' struggles.[3] But just as their foreign policy rhetoric remains resolutely anti-imperialist and anti-neoliberal, while their foreign policy actions are quite the opposite, the Sandinistas maintain a pro-Caribbean Coast autonomy discourse, while subjecting the autonomy process to colonial and imperializing strategies. Hence the government seeks to contain pro-autonomy energies within a nationalist and Sandinista narrative frame, and to marginalize the radical democratic elements that many Miskito and Creole people strive to mobilize. For example, a recent government announcement to celebrate the anniversary of the passing of the autonomy law states rather awkwardly:

> 'Autonomy is how to continue deepening the Revolution here on the Coast, the titling of indigenous lands, the electrification of communities, the improvement of the roads, the improvement of production. It is the whole process that the country is living through (*es todo el proceso que vive el país*), but it has to do with the ethnic and cultural element,' emphasises the coordinator of the Regional Government of the North Caribbean Coast (GRACCN), comrade Carlos Alemán [a Miskito politician]. He reminded us that in the first stage of the Sandinista Revolution, the communities of the Caribbean were being supported, a situation that continues always with *Comandante* Daniel Ortega Saavedra [Ortega Ramírez 2014, our translation].

Such rhetoric notwithstanding, the FSLN has displayed a profound disrespect for indigenous modes of governance. Bernabé Anderson is one of six territorial presidents who have been democratically elected in accordance with autonomy legislation, yet were forcibly removed from power by the regional government without any consultation with constituents. Anderson, who was elected by the community of Wangki Maya in the Río Coco region for a term that was supposed to run until February 2017, told the press in 2015 that 'because we are not Sandinistas, that is why we have been removed from office' (Redacción Central/Trinchera de la Noticia 2015).

The FSLN also passed the interoceanic canal law (Law 840), which gives the government the power to expropriate any territory and displace those who reside there, without consulting with the Creole and indigenous communities who live in

---

[3]See http://www.pgr.gob.ni/index.php/pbgp/54-noticias/1887-nicaragua-celebra-el-dia-de-la-resistencia-indigena-negra-y-popular.

the path of the proposed canal and will lose access to their forests, fishing sites and planting grounds, as well as contact with one another, if it goes ahead (Acosta 2015). Application of Law 840 to the communal lands of indigenous and Afro-descended peoples would seem to contradict and nullify the rights assured to them by Laws 28 and 445. Costeño writer and filmmaker Larry Montenegro Baena (2015a, 2015b) argues that Law 840 constitutes state-led colonialism in the way it neutralises and violates Laws 28 and 445, thus destroying the regional autonomy that has been won through great struggle and sacrifice. The Rama and Kriol Territorial Government, the Communal Creole Government of Bluefields, and the Council of Elders of the Miskito community of Tasbapounie have lodged 31 challenges to Law 840 on the grounds that it is unconstitutional, but these have all been dismissed by the Sandinista-controlled Supreme Court of Justice (Acosta 2014).

The only territory on the Coast still to complete the land titling process is the Black Creole Indigenous Community of Bluefields, where completion has been disrupted by the government because the land occupies part of the route of the proposed canal. Agents acting on behalf of the central government tried to both remove the elected members of the Communal Creole Government of Bluefields from office, and to forcibly evict them from their office space and seize their documents and computers. In an interview, members of the Communal Creole Government told us that their constituents had turned out en masse to protect their offices and forced the police to abandon the attempted eviction. The Sandinista government then tried to force the Communal Creole Government out of office by withdrawing payment on the latter's office space, so members of the community began crowdfunding the rent to maintain the offices. When the Sandinistas' moves against the Bluefields Communal government failed, the Managua government installed an unelected, parallel communal government. According to Dolene Miller, who was one of the democratically elected members of the Creole government as well as the Creole representative at the National Commission for Demarcation and Titling (CONADETI), the central government has worked hard to disrupt both the land claim and the established political structures in Bluefields. She recounted to us that in 2015, the government in Managua forced local Creole leader and FSLN supporter Sidney Francis into her post at CONADETI without an election and that in October 2016, they delivered a title of communal land to the parallel communal government of Bluefields. The title offered by the central government included only 7% of the land that had initially been claimed by the Creole Communal Government of Bluefields. Although the Creole Communal Government's original claim had been accepted by CONADETI in 2010 and established in the published analysis (*diagnóstico*) of 2012 that was required under Law 445, the unelected parallel government nevertheless ignored this history and approved the stripped-back 2016 version of the claim. These matters remained legally unresolved at the time of writing.

The original members of the Communal Creole Government described these processes as 'ideological colonization', and told us they believe that FSLN 'racism is getting worse because we are opening our eyes to our rights and they want to suffocate us'. They believe that the Sandinista government's economic neglect of the region is deliberate and designed to encourage Costeños to migrate to Managua, where they typically end up working in call centres, as a strategy to disconnect them from their communities and traditions and assimilate them into *mestizo* society, an objective that Nicaraguan Creole political theorist Juliet Hooker (2005b) regards as a persistent *mestizo* fantasy of absorption. The Creole leaders asked us, 'How can we talk of a democratic society, a multi-ethnic and pluricultural society when there is political pressure, even political persecution of sectors that do not think like the central government?' The autonomy process on the Caribbean Coast is then subject to government obstruction, much of which takes place through and across the terrain of media and communication. The extensive community support shown for the Creole government reveals, however, the existence of forces that the FSLN did not anticipate and cannot readily control.

3.2 Nicaraguan Mediascapes

It is widely acknowledged that the existence of free, independent and critical media that is able and willing to hold those in power to account is central to a functioning democracy (Sociedad Interamericana de Prensa 1994; Rothschuh Villanueva 2014). There is however ample evidence that the Ortega-Murillo family, in addition to attempting to control all four branches of the government, the army and the police, has gone to extreme measures to undermine press freedom. These measures include the purchase and cooptation of print and broadcast media operations and the centralization and vertical dissemination of official government communications through the Council of Communication and Citizenship led by the first lady, Rosario Murillo. Daily, across official television, radio and Internet, Murillo tells the country how wonderful everything is, emphasising peace, prosperity and employment. Indeed, the FSLN coined a slogan, '*vivir bonito*' (literally 'living nicely'), as a means to euphemize Nicaragua political realities (see Cupples 2014). Nancy Ettlinger and Christopher Hartman (2015: 42), in an analysis of the National Plan for Human Development (PNDH 2012), state that the discourse of *vivir bonito* has a homogenizing effect that reduces Nicaragua's ethnic and cultural diversity to a singular national identity and mobilizes an understanding of indigeneity that is 'colonial' and 'assimilationist'.

The FSLN's vertical communication strategy is accompanied by a *politics of not knowing*, or what Iván Olivares (2015a) calls an 'information blackout'. Olivares notes that the government has all but ceased to collect and publish statistics and development indicators, a move that complicates the delivery of public services, processes of policy formulation, and the informed democratic assessment of the government's performance by the polity. While the government published updated yet highly questionable poverty statistics in October 2015 (the Standard of Living Survey or Encuesta de Medición de Nivel de Vida 2014), it failed to produce other key reports that were due during the same year, including the National Agricultural

Census, the General Population Census, and the Continual Household Survey (Encuesta Continua de Hogares), which measures levels of employment, unemployment and sub-employment.[4] The government has also failed to publish any data on school enrolment levels and health outcomes since 2013, and the Supreme Electoral Council has failed to publish the detailed electoral results of the 2008 municipal elections (Navas and Álvarez 2015). In spite of the environmental threats posed by the advance of the agricultural frontier, the National Forest Inventory that measures forest cover, which should be updated every five years, has not been completed since 2007–08 (Galo Romero 2016). Government and ministry websites are also frequently outdated (Orozco and López 2014). As a result, the government simply has no reliable or credible evidence to support its claims. The requisite information to facilitate informed democratic decision-making has been replaced by pro-government (*oficialista*) rhetoric that serves only to deflect attention from Nicaragua's problems. As Patricia Orozco and Julio López (2014: 174, our translation) write, '[a]n official media dictatorship has been installed in Nicaragua that attempts to demonstrate that the country, its institutions and its population are doing fine'.

Furthermore, the president never gives interviews or holds pres conferences, and ministers and government employees are forbidden from speaking to the media under threat of removal or dismissal from their positions.[5] This ban even extends to government scientists who carry out environmental monitoring of hazard risks. Radio and television licenses and frequencies and state advertising buys are allocated to broadcasters (or withheld or withdrawn from them) in a highly partisan manner. In 1998, when they were in opposition and concerned about the partisan distribution of government advertising budgets by the Liberal government, the FSLN introduced a bill to end this practice. While their majority in the National

[4]With respect to the Standard of Living Survey (*Encuesta de Medición de Nivel de Vida* 2014, available here: http://www.inide.gob.ni/), Enrique Sáenz (2015) notes that the general and extreme poverty lines used by the government in 2015 are the same as they were in 1993, when per capita GDP was one-fifth of the current level. The definition of extreme and general poverty of C$30 a day (around US$1.10) and C$45 a day (around US$1.70), respectively, is less than half of that set by the World Bank, which defines moderate poverty as less than US$4 a day and extreme poverty as less than US$2.25 a day. The alleged fall in poverty can also be attributed more to the reduction in numbers of people per household (which has been fuelled largely by outmigration), to an increase in foreign remittances, and to the growth of the percentage of the population that is of working age, than to Sandinista poverty reduction programmes (see also Olivares 2015b).

[5]In 2007, for example, Margine Gutiérrez, former director of the Nicaraguan Institute of Culture, lost her job when she publicly criticized Daniel Ortega for gifting two original manuscripts authored by Rubén Darío, Nicaragua's most important poet, to Hugo Chávez. In 2013, Sandinista deputy, Xochilt Ocampo, was stripped of her seat in the National Assembly when she abstained from voting on the interoceanic canal (Belli Pereira 2013; *El Nuevo Diario* 2013). At times, the dismissals appear to be enacted to punish minor acts of party disloyalty. In March 2017, two successive secretaries to the municipal council from San Juan del Sur were removed from their positions, the first for attending a school inauguration where the special guest was leading Nicaraguan author and Sandinista dissident, Sergio Ramírez, and the second for appearing on Facebook in a photo with the US ambassador, Laura Dogu (Villareal 2017a, 2017b).

Assembly would make it possible for them to now pass this legislation, they have instead opted to emulate and indeed outdo their predecessors' budgetary favouritisms, thus further undermining media independence and the practices of democracy that require it.

Independent journalists are frequently prevented by the police from covering key events and are subject to multiple forms of harassment by the Sandinistas and their hired *grupos de choque*. Independent media operations have been subjected to heavy-handed audits and the seizure or destruction of equipment. Journalists have also been on the receiving end of death threats and public physical attacks while doing their jobs (see *La Prensa* 2015; Cenidh Nicaragua 2015). Foreign journalists have also been obstructed. For instance, in December 2014, a Belgian photojournalist, Michéle Sennesael, who had been filming anti-canal protests, was deported from Nicaragua after police raided her hotel and seized her photographs and equipment. In February 2016, Carlos Ponce, director of the Latin American office of the human rights organization, Freedom House, was denied entry to Nicaragua when he attempted to travel there to participate in a series of meetings with civil society organizations. This denial came shortly after Freedom House had published its 2015 annual report, which noted that, 'unlike other Central American countries, where criminal gangs, political violence and systemic corruption are the principal threats to democracy, in Nicaragua the main threat is political and institutional domination of the Sandinista party' (quoted in Miranda Aburto 2016). After his removal, Ponce tweeted that expelling him from Nicaragua would not prevent people from knowing that Ortega's government is authoritarian. Nevertheless, the actions of the Nicaraguan government have produced a state of generalized fear, practices of censorship and self-censorship, and therefore constriction of spaces for democratic dialogue, debate and deliberation (for detailed discussion of the state of press freedom in Nicaragua, see Orozco and López 2014; Rothschuh Villanueva 2014; Navarrete 2015).

The Nicaraguan television broadcasting system is now largely in duopoly that in the view of some analysts (see, e.g., Carballo et al. 2014; Orozco 2015) violates Article 68. The Ortega-Murillo family own channels 4, 6, 8, 13 and 22, while Mexican media entrepreneur, Angel González, controls channels 2, 9, 10 and 11 (also known as TV Red). These channels make up 90 per cent of the terrestrial broadcasters in the country. Furthermore, the Ortega-Murillo family and González own more than 100 Nicaraguan radio stations. There is now only one nationwide terrestrial TV broadcaster in Nicaragua that does not belong to the duopoly: Channel 12. Channel 12 is owned by a conservative Nicaraguan family and carries a well-respected, independent, weekly current affairs show, *Esta Semana* (hosted by Carlos Fernando Chamorro), which was previously broadcast on Channel 8 before the latter was purchased by the Ortega-Murillo family. In addition, there are three national cable channels, 14, 15 and 23, that are not part of the duopoly. However, 15 and 23 are owned by declared Sandinista supporters, and 14 is owned by the superwealthy Pellas family, which has benefited from the Sandinista government's failures to respond to public pressures, protests and demands for action in the face of a chronic epidemic of occupational kidney disease among sugar cane workers employed by the Pellas family in Chinandega, more than 20,000 of whom have died from the illness over a period of two decades (see Salinas Maldonado 2014; Chedekel 2015).[6] Channel 15, also known as *100% Noticias*, is a popular news channel with a sensationalist focus on urban crime, violence and conflict. It enjoys substantial advertising revenue and does not openly criticise the government. It does however, cover a variety of everyday conflicts and antagonisms involving low-income communities in the capital. Channel 15 is also the most popular online on-demand channel in Nicaragua. In 2016, Channel 15 took over the show *Café con Voz* from Channel 23. *Café con Voz* is a programme that does provide some limited space for critical political debate. *Café con Voz* is also available online at both the Channel 15 website and on YouTube, and is also broadcast via several regional radio stations. As a result, the reach and 'spreadability' (or sharing potential; see Jenkins, Ford and Green 2013) of its reports are considerably enhanced.

Until recently, Nicaragua had two independent daily national newspapers, the centre-left *El Nuevo Diario*, established in 1980, and the centre-right *La Prensa*, which was established in 1926 and is owned by the Chamorro family. In 2011, *El Nuevo Diario* was purchased by Banpro (a private banking group) and is now widely considered to be a co-opted publication that does not challenge the Sandinista party line. This leaves the centre-right *La Prensa* as the only remaining independent national daily print publication. *La Prensa* takes a very critical line towards the government, and always refers to Daniel Ortega as 'the unconstitutional president' (*el presidente inconstitucional*), a reference to the fact that his ostensible re-election violates the Nicaraguan Constitution. In addition to *La Prensa*, there are two online publications: *Confidencial* (an independent newspaper) and *Trinchera de la Noticia* (which is jointly owned by former right-wing president Arnoldo Alemán and a former subeditor of *Barricada*, which had been the official Sandinista newspaper during the Revolution).[7] These are both fairly independent organs that avail themselves of the fact that the state makes no effort to restrict access to any part of the Internet, and so they regularly publish content that is critical of the Sandinista government.[8] While Internet connectivity is much lower in Nicaragua

[6]The Boston University School of Public Health has been investigating this epidemic since 2009, and published results in 2015 showing that "occupational factors" likely play a role in the epidemic, but that their study "did not find support for the hypothesis that agricultural chemicals are a causal agent for kidney disease. Instead, among field-workers, agrichemical applicators, who have the most direct contact with chemicals, were found to experience the smallest decline in kidney function." However, the BU researchers also wrote that the use of agricultural chemicals "remain[s] an important hypothesis and warrant[s] further study" (Chedekel 2015).

[7]*Confidencial* publishes a weekly print version that is circulated in Managua. *Barricada* folded in 1998.

[8]At the start of the 2016 election campaign, there was an attempt to control social media interventions, a move that was roundly condemned and rapidly abandoned (López 2016).

than in other parts of Latin America, it is growing rapidly, and 'connected' Nicaraguans make heavy use of social media sites such as Facebook.[9]

Television is as heavily controlled at the regional broadcasting scale in Nicaragua as are the country's nationwide channels. Several TV and radio stations, especially those that reported on electoral fraud during the 2008 elections, have been closed down (Orozco and López 2014). This is a situation that shapes the struggle for autonomy and land rights on the Caribbean Coast in significant ways. The region has a long tradition of highly participatory and democratic community radio offering regular open mike sessions that enable community members to come into the station to speak on air about the failures of political authorities to fulfil their responsibilities to the public (see Glynn and Cupples 2011). This tradition has been undermined as repression and censorship have intensified. Community media is seen as particularly important in the region due to the ongoing stigmatization of the Coast in mainstream media. Many Costeño broadcasters told us that they are motivated to work in local media to counter the stereotypical narratives and representations of the Coast that dominate the national Nicaraguan media. They complain that mainstream media are fixated on *sucesos*: negative stories of drug trafficking, crime, political instability, natural disasters, violent conflict and road accidents. These *sucesos* reproduce and reinforce the dominant colonial and imperializing meanings and discourses that *mestizos* attach to the Coast. Ironically, these *sucesos* thus represent Caribbean Nicaragua for inhabitants of the Pacific region in a fashion that is structurally similar to the way 'first world' media have historically represented the 'third world' as a whole for their audiences. Costeño Community broadcasters we interviewed described their work as 'supporting municipal and regional development' and 'giving a voice to those who do not have a voice', and told us that, 'we feel part of the people'. One Miskito journalist said that he and his colleagues are 'scrutinizers, spokespeople for the lower classes, intermediaries between power and the people' (Joel EMC 2016). They strive to both broaden the repertoire of discourses, narratives and representations through which the Coast is understood, and to contextualise, complicate and contest those generated and circulated through the national mainstream media. They also frequently emphasise the educative and interculturalizing roles of community media, so to promote greater mutual understanding between the region's diverse cultures and the formation of Costeño solidarities.

Community media are viewed by some broadcasters as instrumental for securing legal rights and achieving the implementation of Law 445. Indigenous and Afro-descendant activists and community leaders on the Caribbean Coast who

[9]According to interworldstats.com, 27% of Nicaraguans had access to the Internet in 2015, compared with a Central American average of 46.8%. In 2016, access to the Internet by Nicaraguans had risen to 31.8% (against a Central American regional average of 53%), according to the same source (accessed 9 Dec. 2016).

began to draw on the new legal frameworks to advance the autonomy process assert that one key drawback to mobilizing the population around both autonomy in general and demarcation, in particular, was a generalized lack of historical awareness and a sense of inferiority among the Costeño population. In order to produce the analysis (*diagnóstico*) mandated by stage one of Law 445, claimants had to carry out in-depth research on historical events, including the historically persistent denial of rights in the region. This research activity proved to be an important mobilising and awareness-raising process that affirmed the urgency of the situation (see for example Comunidad Negra Creole Indígena de Bluefields 2012). Community media played an important role in supporting the Costeño recovery and revival of local histories.

The political implications of cultural recognition in law are multifaceted and depend largely on a range of conjunctural factors. It is possible, as Michael Watts (2003: 25) remarks, that '[o]nce law enshrines cultural identity as the basis for political identity, it necessarily converts ethnicity into a potent force'. Hale's (2005) work demonstrates, however, that under conditions of 'neoliberal multiculturalism', cultural rights are all too frequently limited and domesticated by hegemonic forces. Nevertheless, there is some evidence that as they negotiated dominant *mestizajes* and the autonomy process, the counter-hegemonic force of Costeño politics was intensified rather than calmed, as the *mestizo* politicians perhaps hoped it would be. The withdrawal of state advertising from community TV and radio operations on the Caribbean Coast was one way to calm the political ferment in the region by driving some of the most explicitly activist programming off the air. One radio station, Kabu Yula, whose owner we interviewed in 2009, collapsed shortly thereafter when it lost 13 of its 15 sponsors as a result of the state pressuring advertisers not to support the station (Cupples, Glynn and Lee forthcoming).[10] It was reported in October 2016 that Radio Zinica in Bluefields removed a programme from its schedule on direct orders from the government (Lacayo Ortiz 2016). Other stations that engage in overt political activism have had their broadcasting licenses suspended, their electricity supply cut off, their vehicles damaged or their transmitters destroyed. Some broadcasters are thus encouraged, as one Creole radio station owner told us, to focus on baseball and music and to avoid political debate (though it should be noted that baseball and music are also important activators of regional identity and solidarities).

In addition to outright repression and the deliberate production of economic precarity among broadcasters on the Caribbean Coast through the withdrawal of state advertising, the Sandinistas have also funded rival television and radio stations in the region, in an attempt to reduce the audiences for grassroots community media operations. There are now three local cable community television stations in Bilwi, the capital of the North Caribbean region. *Canal* 5, created, funded and managed by local university URACCAN, was the first community television channel on the

[10]The closure of Kabu Yula was also reported in a WikiLeaks cable. See www.wikileaks.org/plusd/cables/09MANAGUA959_a.html.

Coast. It broadcasts programmes on local community issues and works in support of indigenous and Creole cultural and political revitalization (see Glynn and Cupples 2011; Cupples and Glynn 2014a). In 2008, a group of *Canal* 5 broadcasters broke away to form their own independent channel, TV7, which is funded mostly by advertising along with some NGO support. These two channels broadcast in all of the languages spoken in the region and play an important role in promoting autonomy and cultural citizenship. In addition, the region has a number of important popular community radio stations, probably the most outspoken of which are *Radio Caribe* in Bilwi and *Radio La Costeñisima* in Bluefields. In an effort to compete with local grassroots content on both radio and television, the central Nicaraguan government has created *Canal* 22, designated 'the channel of autonomy', and also funds Radio Bilwi Stereo in Bilwi in the North Caribbean and Radio Bluefields Stereo in Bluefields in the South Caribbean. These channels are much better resourced than the region's community media, have high-power transmission capabilities, and enjoy privileged access to information from the central and regional governments, in violation of the Law of Access to Public Information (Romero 2015a). The national politics of not knowing is replicated at the regional level as a consequence of these media acquisitions. As director of Miskito radio station *Yapti Tasba*, Juan Herbacio, told the Nicaraguan Centre for Human Rights (CENIDH),

> as journalists in the region, we suffer persecution in the sense of censorship of information. If we go to the Regional Council to ask them why they have not endorsed the territorial leaders that have been democratically elected by the community, they refuse to give us any information [Cenidh Nicaragua 2015, our translation].

Our interviewees in both the North and South Caribbean revealed the constraints under which they operate, which have been in place for a number of years but have intensified more recently. Let us provide a few examples.

In order to facilitate the participation of the Bluefields Creole population in the demarcation process, the Creole government began to rent a space on Radio Rhythm to broadcast a weekly programme on black history. Entitled *Demarcation Now*, it ran every Saturday for two hours and contained 'capsules about history, rights and law'. In an interview, representatives from the Creole government described the ways in which they were forced off the air, which included pressure by the Nicaraguan government on the owner of the station to stop broadcasting the show, and attempted forcible eviction by the police during a broadcast. The station owner eventually gave into the pressure, so that when the broadcasters turned up to present their show one day, they found themselves locked out. They then sought a space on Bluefields Stereo, the radio station controlled by the Regional Government. They were asked to submit an official proposal, but never received a response, and view this non-response as a violation of their constitutional rights. They now broadcast their show on *Radio Siempre Joven*, which they viewed as a compromise, given that this station has a much smaller signal range and until recently was not available on the Internet. After broadcasting only locally for six years, however, in 2017 they began simulcasting through Facebook, which has enabled them to reach a much larger audience. According to Dolene Miller, there have been repeated attempts to buy the space occupied by *Demarcation Now*, but at the time of writing, the weekly broadcast nevertheless continues. Growing awareness of historical Costeño rights has thus both facilitated and complicated the implementation of Law 445, and it has become apparent that merely talking about black history on the radio is understood as a threat by the Sandinista power-bloc. As one member of the Creole government explained to us, when the communities began to elect their communal governments in the wake of the enactment of Law 445,

> at first, neither the Liberals nor the Sandinistas did put much mind to it. They were like, 'look at the little Indians and black people defending their customs and traditions, no problem.' But when they realized that the demarcation process means that communities are owners of the resources and they cannot dispose of them as they did before, they need the consent of the community, they realized they had made a mistake by recognising historical rights. The community, the owners of the land have to be consulted and the consultation has to be free, prior and informed. No exploitation of resources such as the canal project can happen if they do not consent.

The circulation of black histories is especially challenging to the modes of coloniality that *mestizo* ideologies engender. The discourses of black regional histories circulate an alternative sense of the Nicaraguan nation-state, which is thus constituted not as a source of pride, but rather as a beneficiary of violent annexation and an agent of cultural erasure and of the repression of black and indigenous knowledges and languages. Moreover, the region's black historical discourses challenge dominant Eurocentric geopolitical imaginaries of indigenous and black Costeños as 'people without a history' (Mignolo 2005: xii). Such imaginaries are the products of 'white ignorance', which is, as Charles Mills (1997, 2015) shows, 'a type of epistemology' and 'a sort of useful non-knowledge' that requires 'ever vigilant understanding of what not to know' (Gross and McGoey 2015: 5). We should note the links between the epistemology of white ignorance and the silencing of black historical discourses, which must be understood as structural rather than conspiratorial (Trouillet 1995: 106; Gould 1998: 12). It is these structural links that lead to the political scrutinization and suppression of black and indigenous people's media that seeks to increase knowledge of both past and present forces of coloniality.

One Miskito radio broadcaster described suffering harassment just after Hurricane Felix in 2007, but also being defended by listeners. The ways in which Costeños often mobilize to defend their community media operations when they are threatened demonstrates the important role they play. It reveals the communities' affective investments in their media, and suggests their role in the enactment of horizontality and reciprocity, and in blurring the 'boundaries between emissaries and receptors' (Zibechi 2010: 62). This broadcaster told us the following:

> We realized after Hurricane Felix that there was a lot of corruption associated with the distribution of donations that were coming in. The donations weren't reaching their intended destinations and the people that were receiving them were putting their own spin on events (*hacían su propaganda*). Even though money was coming in from other countries, they were putting their own spin on it. So we started opposing these things on the radio, talking about all this injustice, and they tried to close us down. They even cut off our

> power. They actually tried to cut our power so we couldn't broadcast. In the moment we went on air to start our programme, they ordered our electricity to be cut. We had no idea, but somehow the people knew that they were coming to cut off our power, so they came and seized the vehicles of the electricity company. They turned over the vehicle and they even removed the gear stick. It was all a manoeuvre. They ended up blowing nineteen pieces of equipment in total. Our computers, our satellite system, everything. The transmitter, the console, everything, and it's taken us years to get it all replaced.

Another broadcaster described receiving phone calls and messages during a programme dealing with the views of those living in the path of the proposed canal:

> The programme hadn't finished when people who are part of the government who were watching it started calling me and sending me messages. I had to sincerely apologise out of fear they would close my company. I live off this. I look after my family with it and employ people. And if I as a media operator have this fear, you can imagine how afraid ordinary people are. There is fear in the population, especially among those who live along the canal route.

Georgina Vargas, a Miskito freelance journalist, has received death threats that she has reported to human rights organizations and independent media. Vargas originally worked for *Canal* 22, the government-owned local channel, where she was a reporter for a Miskitu language news programme entitled *Tawan Bilibaikra* (*The Voice of the People*). It was a difficult job because reporters were prohibited from interviewing elected politicians. She was fired when she did an interview with the mayor. She then rented a paid space on TV7 and began to broadcast an indigenous rights programme in Miskitu entitled *Tawan Inangka* (*The Clamour of the People*). However, TV7 was threatened with closure if it did not remove Vargas' programme from the air, so she decided to resign rather than endanger the group of young Creole and Miskito mediamakers who run the station.

On 30 October 2015, radio broadcaster Juan Herbacio, who has also received death threats via his cell phone, was physically attacked by a Sandinista mob that assaulted him while he was shopping at the supermarket. He has also received messages from people threatening to burn down his radio station. Herbacio told *La Prensa* in an interview that 'because we are members of an indigenous organisation that does not support the FSLN, they threaten to burn down the radio station' (*La Prensa* 2015b). Herbacio's story and those of the others that we have mentioned, lead us to conclude that producing black and indigenous media has become a dangerous activity in Nicaragua, and that the power-bloc's media strategy has been devastating for press freedom in the country.

In an influential essay addressing media in Great Britain, Stuart Hall (1981: 28) wrote that 'a sort of racist "common sense" has become pervasive in our society. And the media frequently work from this common sense, taking it as their base-line without questioning it. We need, urgently, to consider the ways in which… we can… begin to construct an anti-racist common sense. This task of making anti-racist ideas popular is and must be part of a wider democratic struggle'. For Hall (1981: 33), racism is an ideological practice that, like white ignorance, 'has its own specific way of working' and is 'generated, produced and reproduced in specific settings (sites)—especially in the apparatuses of ideological production which "produce" social meanings and distribute them throughout society, like the media'. Like all ideological practices, the production and circulation of meanings around racial difference are subject to ongoing struggle and contestation, and as Gramsci showed, such contestation can easily slide from the realm of a struggle for common sense into that of coercion and the application of force (see Hall 1996: 426). The intimidation and suppression of Black Creole and Miskito mediamakers and activists suggest an instance of such slippage from the ideological struggle for common sense and consent to the activation of coercive forces. It suggests the application of powers that extend beyond the realm of 'symbolic annihilation' inflicted on non-white populations in Western media (Tuchman 1972; McGregor and Te Awa 1996). It is telling that in August 2015, to mark the upcoming International Day of the Journalist on 8 September, Miskito reporter Jerry López produced a short documentary broadcast on TV7 in which local journalists and mediamakers on the Caribbean Coast described the climate of intimidation and necessary self-censorship in which they have been driven to operate (see Joel EMC 2016).

As Hall (1996: 426) notes, 'domination and coercion can maintain the ascendancy of a particular class over a society. But its "reach" is limited. It has to rely consistently on coercive means, rather than the winning of consent'. Meanwhile, within the context of the emergent media environment in Nicaragua, alternative spaces are appearing within which to conduct struggles for cultural citizenship and for the formation of alternative modes of popular, anti-racist common sense. Castells (2007: 244) asserts that in the network society, 'media are the space of power making, not the space of power holding'. Similarly, Daniel Dayan (2009: 20) identifies the ways in which the emergence of a 'multitiered public sphere' associated with digitalization and ubiquitous, multiplatform, convergent media is giving rise to a 'globally sensitive battlefield' upon which contesting mediated engagements with the same events are generating 'so many conflicting versions' of things in 'so many competing media'. These developments are participating in and contributing to the profound conjunctural crisis in Nicaragua, just as they helped disrupt the Bush administration's strategies of media control and 'perception management' in relation to the Iraq War (Mirzoeff 2005) and Hurricane Katrina (Cupples and Glynn 2014b). In Nicaragua today, those who are removed from or silenced in mainstream and community media spaces do not cease to broadcast, but rather shift their focus to other sites and opportunities, and have turned in particular to social media such as Facebook, Twitter and YouTube. Although the Sandinistas have, according to our informants, begun to deploy an 'ideological brigade' of young online agents tasked with disrupting and trolling anti-government activists, the latter have thus far managed, broadly speaking, to operate beyond the grasp of the FSLN.

Chapter 4
Crisis and Conflict on the Caribbean Coast

Abstract This chapter explores media responses to the current crisis on the Caribbean Coast and setbacks to struggles for land rights within the region. It provides a detailed overview of conflicts in the North Caribbean, particularly those involving the violent actions of illegal settlers who are accelerating the growth of insecurity and environmental degradation. It also outlines the ongoing struggles of the Rama-Kriol people in the South Caribbean against the interoceanic canal that threatens their lands and communities. This chapter deploys Boaventura de Sousa Santos' concept of the 'sociology of absences' to explore the Nicaraguan government's inaction, indifference and deceptions, as well as the grassroots production of visibility by digitally equipped citizens.

Keywords Conflict · Deforestation · Interoceanic canal · YouTube
Facebook · Memes

On the Caribbean Coast of Nicaragua, as noted, the tensions surrounding the presence of illegal settlers on communal lands and the obstacles in the way of completing the demarcation process have been high for a number of years. The temporary FSLN-YATAMA electoral alliance forged in 2006 collapsed as the demarcation and land-titling process gained momentum. Even as land titles were granted, *colonos* continued to migrate from the Pacific to the Coast, where they cleared forests, illegally sold the valuable timber, brought in cattle, built homes, and engaged in illegal land trades supported by falsified documents. Since 2010, the government has received notice of 339 cases of invasion and illegal titling of indigenous communal property in the Bosawas region. These cases have been meticulously documented and mapped by the territorial governments and presented to the police in Siuna and Bonanza. Despite interventions from National Assembly deputies urging both the national chief of police and the president to intervene, absolutely nothing has been done (see Navas 2015b).

The environmental destruction created by the arrival of *terceros* in the region has been colossal. According to Mayangna leader, Alisio Genaro, in 1997, the Bosawas forest, a designated UNESCO Biosphere Reserve, had more than two million

J. Cupples and K. Glynn, *Shifting Nicaraguan Mediascapes*,
SpringerBriefs in Latin American Studies,
https://doi.org/10.1007/978-3-319-64319-9_4

Fig. 4.1 What would you do with $45,000. Would you plant one of these? Or would you plant 195,000 of these? *Source:* Bacanalnica.com

hectares of protected forest and was home to 7000 indigenous people. By 2010, the population had increased to 25,000, the vast majority of whom were *colonos* from the Pacific, and the forest was reduced to 832,237 hectares. By 2013, the number of *colonos* had increased to 40,000 (see Silva 2015). Nicaraguan geographer and presidential advisor, Jaime Incer Barquero, has drawn attention to the failure of the state to protect the putatively protected areas and to the ongoing tendency to grant further concessions for logging at highly vulnerable sites (Cruz 2016). The presence of so many *colonos* and their cattle has also led to a dramatic reduction in wild animals, such as *guardatinajas* (pacas) and *guatusas* (agoutis), which are key sources of bushmeat for the local inhabitants. The inability to farm securely and the disappearance of these mammals have intensified hunger and malnutrition in the region. At the end of 2015, Sandinista media announced that the Ministry of the Environment and Natural Resources (MARENA) would plant windbreaks consisting of 400,000 trees in Chinandega, León, Managua and Masaya, but made no mention of reforestation plans for Bosawas (Álvarez 2016a). The ongoing destruction of Bosawas, and the failure of the central government to enact measures to protect it, have led to the creation of an active environmental movement, Misión Bosawas.[1] Many Nicaraguans have taken to social media to decry the government's failures both to prevent indiscriminate deforestation and to reforest any affected areas, while it nevertheless and with perverse irony pours millions of dollars into the erection of decorative metallic trees in the capital city of Managua (see Fig. 4.1).

By 2015, tensions in the RACCN had escalated, especially in the communities around Waspam. The *colonos* are well armed, and by mid-year had become more

[1]See misionbosawas.org/ and www.facebook.com/MisionBOSAWAS/timeline.

violent. They had begun to destroy indigenous homes and crops and to prevent community members from accessing their fields. Miskitos have pointed out that many of the *colonos* possess military grade weaponry such as AK-47s, which has prompted suspicions that they are being supplied by the army (Flores 2015). Some Miskitos began to take up arms in order to defend themselves and retaliate. Many others lacking food and security became internal refugees and were displaced to the regional capital of Bilwi, or to Honduras. By September 2015, 800 families had been displaced, 60 homes had been destroyed, 15 people had been killed and several more were injured (Silva 2015). Despite the threats the situation posed to the lives of Nicaraguan citizens, security forces have either remained absent or have acted against the legal owners of the lands rather than against the *colonos*. The president of the Miskito community of Wangki Twi, Cornelio Tebas, told *La Prensa* that Daniel Ortega is trying to eliminate indigenous peoples in Nicaragua. Tebas asserts that

> the government's aim is to put an end to us, to put an end to indigenous peoples. Here the leaders of the Sandinista Front defend the rights of the *colonos* at all costs; we practically don't have a president, we don't feel Nicaraguan; we don't have a government, we don't have anyone to protect us. We feel alone because here the army and the police attack the indigenous peoples [Chamorro 2015a, our translation].

On 15 September 2015, Romel Constantino Washington, the vice-president of Wangki Twi, Obencio Downs Peralta, president of the community's Youth Council, and Rossman Flores Gonzales, a representative of the Council of Elders of Bilwi, were seriously injured in an army ambush while attempting to deliver food and humanitarian assistance to families under siege from *colonos*' violence (Chamorro 2015b; Front Line Defenders 2015). Shortly after denouncing these human rights abuses, Constantino was accused by the FSLN in pro-Sandinista media of participating in the illegal sale of communal property (see La Voz del Sandinismo 2015). On 17 December 2015, *colonos* attacked the communities of Wisconsin and Esperanza, which resulted in three deaths, three injuries, and three kidnappings from these communities (Romero 2015b). Independent media began to publish headlines such as 'Hunger and Abandonment in RAAN Communities' (Navarro 2015), 'Government Denies Indigenous Crisis to the IACHR' (Romero et al. 2015; IACHR refers to the Inter-American Commission on Human Rights), and 'Indigenous Conflicts Ignored by *Orteguista* Deputees' (Álvarez 2016), thus capturing both the violence and suffering in the communities and the Sandinista government's strategies for the production of indigenous non-existence. The entire municipality of Waspam, which includes 75,000 inhabitants and spans more than 8,000 square kilometres, has only 30 or so police officers (Silva 2015), which is fewer than the number employed to defend the presidential home in Managua. On 3 October 2015, the Centre for Justice and Human Rights on the Atlantic Coast of Nicaragua (CEJUDHCAN) took the case of Waspam to the Inter-American Commission on Human Rights. The Commission acknowledged the gravity and urgency of the situation and granted cautious measures in favour of four communities, Esperanza, Santa Clara, Wisconsin and Francia Sirpi, which all belong to the territory of Wangki Twi Tasba Raya (CEJIL 2015).

Boaventura de Sousa Santos' (2004) concept of the sociology of absences is useful for thinking about the ways in which Costeños are challenging the attempts by the power-bloc to shut down counter-hegemonic alternatives and restrict what exists. De Sousa Santos asserts that hegemonic forces actively produce non-existence through a privileging of five monocultures: (scientific/Eurocentric) knowledge, (linear) time, (racial) classification, (global/universal) scale, and (capitalist and market-driven) productivity. Through decolonial struggle, these monocultures can, however, be replaced by ecologies that endorse and make visible alternative knowledges, temporalities and economic systems, that replace hierarchies with recognition, and that reverse the scalar logics of globalisation. De Sousa Santos (2004: 240) notes that 'in each of the five domains, the objective of the sociology of absences is to disclose, and give credit to, the diversity and multiplicity of social practices in opposition to the exclusive credibility of hegemonic practices'. The Sandinista power-bloc's attempts to establish a monopoly on credibility is thwarted by ongoing contestation over territorial rights, cultural identities, environmental resources, neoliberal megaprojects and the defense of non-destructive practices. As a result, an ecological counter-hegemony is emerging—albeit one that is partial, fragmented and hybrid—thus laying the terrain for what de Sousa Santos refers to as a sociology of emergences that 'enlarge the signs of possible future experiences' (p. 241). This is made possible not only by the dispersal of power, but also by the forms of affective engagement, connectivity and knowledge circulation facilitated through mediated interaction. We might say that Costeño mediamakers are themselves engaged in forms of a vernacular practice of the sociology of absences and emergences.

Given the urgency of the situation, territorial and communal leaders and human rights defenders are anxious to complete the demarcation process. As Law 445 did not specify how the final stage (*saneamiento*) of demarcation is to be carried out, these leaders and activists appealed to the authorities in Managua to come to the negotiating table in an attempt to reach agreement on the process. These efforts were, however, met with complete silence from the Sandinista government. In the face of this silence, CEJUDCHAN and community leaders produced a manual with an accompanying popular version that recommended a workable process. They then travelled to Managua to present their proposal to the relevant authorities. In the face of the consistent and repeated non-response by the Sandinistas, the black and indigenous leaders used video cameras to document the latest phase of their struggle and uploaded the footage to YouTube. The result is a 14-minute film that captures the situation they face (Cejudhcan derechos humanos 2015a). Along with their supporters, the presidents of the 23 black and indigenous territories travelled the long and arduous journey by bus from Managua in order to meet with government officials at the Crowne Plaza, a central Managua hotel. However, the officials failed to materialize. The video therefore consists of a room full of empty chairs bearing the names of the members of the Nicaraguan government who refused to appear (see Fig. 4.2). In place of the absent Sandinistas is an explanation

Fig. 4.2 Empty chairs
Source: Cejudhcan derechos humanos (2015a)

of Law 445, including the legal requirement that the state work with the territories to fulfil the process of *saneamiento*. Participants tell the camera of the urgency of the situation, of the deepening threats to their ways of life, and of the serious environmental destruction enacted through the ever-intensifying presence of *terceros* in their territories. They then denounce the situation to the national media. The video thus draws attention to the black and indigenous leaders' failed attempts to engage in a horizontal and inter-epistemic dialogue with government authorities, and reveals that Nicaragua is not a space of democracy and social justice in which autonomy is flourishing, but rather one in which black and indigenous rights, and even attempts at dialogue, are denied. The activist filmmakers conclude with a march for justice in which their banners articulate the presence of the *terceros* to the government's failure to address the issue, and to the problem of the proposed canal, thus casting all three as products of a common matrix of coloniality.

As Paul Adams (2015) shows in his discussion of the media geographies surrounding the conspicuous absence of Chinese political prisoner Liu Xiaobo from the 2010 Nobel Peace Prize ceremony in Norway, images of empty chairs can convey multiple messages on different levels at once. Like the Oslo City Hall discussed by Adams, the Crowne Plaza in Managua became 'a container full of witnesses to a very particular absence' that was used to 'broadcast a particular message regarding human rights, freedom of speech, justice, and peace' (p. 315). In this way, the missing bodies of Nicaraguan government officials who may wish to communicate nothing at all, end up being made to communicate rather a lot about both their attitudes towards Caribbean Coast autonomy and about the acceptability to the subordinated of these attitudes. The immediate witnesses in this instance included the Costeño participants attempting to engage in peaceful dialogue, and the members of the independent media who joined them. This witness base was numerically expanded and spatially extended, though, once video footage of the event was shared on YouTube. Hence the event became spatially unbound and available for articulation (in the sense of linkage) to other places. In the process, the place meanings of Nicaragua as a site of democracy, which the government attempts routinely to stabilize, are similarly rearticulated (in the sense of resignification) to express (and oppose) the denial of black and indigenous rights and attempts at dialogue. As John Fiske (2016a: 230) writes, 'making visible… is a form of counter-power, and the knowledge it produces and circulates works to construct and validate a counter-reality'.

Since completing and uploading this video, CEJUDHCAN has made several more that also produce knowledges that the Sandinistas seek to consign to the category of the unknown, including one with English subtitles that strives to circulate these knowledges as a means of generating new transnational solidarities (Cejudhcan derechos humanos 2015b). Their work in this area is fascinating and pioneering. In July 2015, 50 community members from the territory of Wangki Twi Tasba Raya embarked on a field trip with members of CEJUDHCAN to determine the number of *terceros* present in their territory and to produce videographic documentation of the extent of ongoing natural resource destruction there. Their video (Cejudhcan derechos humanos 2015c) reveals the tragic felling of huge quantities of trees, the presence of cattle, and the pollution of rivers (see Fig. 4.3). A CEJUDHCAN technician explains in the film that this visibly rampant forest clearance was done not with machetes and axes but with chain saws, thus indicating

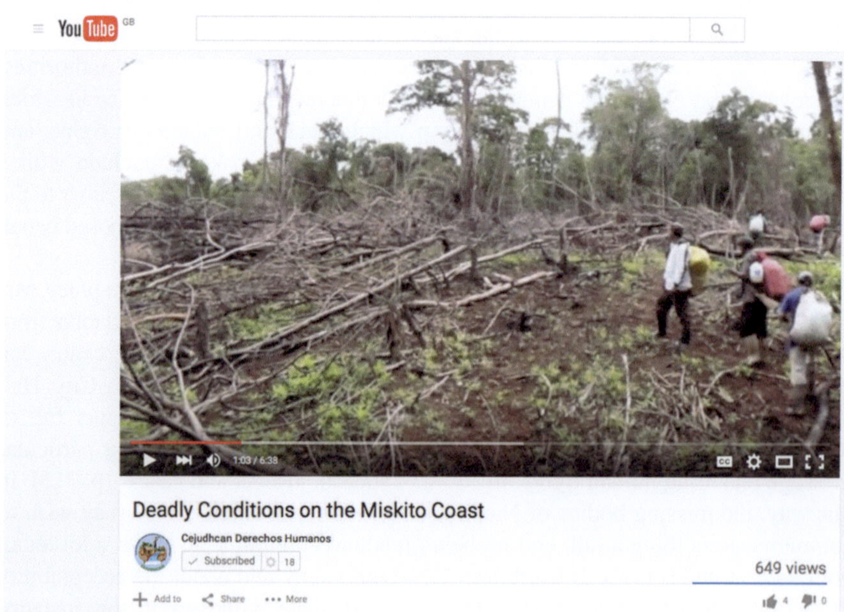

Fig. 4.3 Environmental destruction in Waspam
Source: Cejudhcan derechos humanos 2015c

either that the *colonos* are not impoverished *campesinos*, or that if they are, they have been provided with expensive machinery by others in support of their efforts to colonize these indigenous communal lands. During filming, community members encounter a *colono* who tells them that he purchased 100 *manzanas* (70 hectares) of land for C$300,000 (about £7000), and had already completely clear-felled 45 of these. In this way, these filmmakers use cameras to bring into knowledge that which would otherwise go unseen and thus unknown: compelling evidence of illegal sales of their lands, and of extreme environmental and biodiversity destruction. What is unknown cannot be acted upon, so the production of knowledge is a source of mobilization. Furthermore, knowledge and the networks through which it is often formed in the new communication environment can have affective dimensions that catalyse and intensify such mobilization. Tiziana Terranova (2004: 156) observes that new digital networks offer the potential to facilitate forms of 'political experimentation, where the overall dynamics of a capillary communication milieu can be used productively as a kind of common ground' that forms the conditions of possibility for the production and advancement of a 'common *passion* giving rise to a *distributed movement* able to displace the limits and terms within which the political constitution of the future is played out'.

Inspired perhaps by the new media visibility that CEJUDHCAN has brought to the conflict, a group of young Miskito men from the community of Francia Sirpi wrote, performed and filmed a song about 'the territorial invasion by the colonos' and their struggle for justice (Cejudhcan derechos humanos 2015d). These performers are shown gathered on their ancestral lands and singing about the 'many problems and situations' that afflicted Francia Sirpi in 2015, including the inability to farm or safely cross the river, the disappearance of wildlife and the widespread deforestation of cedar and mahogany trees (see Fig. 4.4). Their song describes an encounter with a *colono* who flees into the mountains in fear when confronted, and entreats the 'authorities' to 'support us, support us'. The song appropriates the

Fig. 4.4 Young men of Francia Sirpi
Source: Cejudhcan derechos humanos 2015d

language of Nicaragua's revolutionary past in its appeal to an imagined '*Comandante*: brave man, where are you?' The singers thus implicitly reject the *mestizo* masculinism of Daniel Ortega's latest incarnation as a counterrevolutionary strongman (*caudillo*) who calls upon the nation's revolutionary history only to serve his own narrow interests. In this way, these singers engage in a struggle for the meanings of Nicaraguan revolution, and seek to extend those meanings to include and to advance their own struggles for indigenous land rights against an illegal colonial invasion. When they call 'where are you?' these Miskito singers indict the *mestizo* state for its failures to implement the law and uphold security, and they subvert the *mestizo* norm against which the indigenous/Creole identity is repeatedly marked as other. The boys' appeal to Nicaragua's revolutionary past is encoded in what John Fiske (2016b: 138) calls the 'videolow' mode of a cell phone recording: a 'low-technicity' that is 'low in clarity but high in authenticity', for it stems from 'the videolow's apparently continuous or metonymic relationship with the experiential truths (or 'true' experiences) of the socially disempowered'. This sense of videographic authenticity is both enhanced by and reinforces the boys' evocations of Nicaragua's revolutionary history and tradition.

In 2016 and 2017, the president of CEJUDHCAN, Lottie Cunningham, and other staff began to receive death threats via text messages as well as CEJUDHCAN's Facebook page, which suggests that their work was indeed drawing attention to the state's failure to protect life and territory in the North Caribbean. In March 2017, the threats to Lottie's life became the subject of an urgent appeal by the Dublin-based human rights organisation Front Line Defenders, whereby they urged the Nicaraguan authorities to 'carry out an immediate, thorough and impartial investigation into the threats against CEJUDHCAN's staff and other human rights defenders in Nicaragua, with a view to publishing the results and bringing those responsible to justice in accordance with international standards'.[2] While many, but by no means all, Nicaraguans are afraid to speak out in support of Lottie's work, international solidarity is growing. At the same time, Front Line Defenders also nominated Francisca Ramírez Torres, who has also suffered threats and harassment as a result of her anti-canal activism, for the 2017 Award for Human Rights Defenders at Risk.

Other Costeños have also been uploading material on the recent conflicts to YouTube. As a result, media content is moving from locally available community channels to globally accessible online spaces, thus increasing its circulation and its potential for transmediation across technologies and platforms. In this way, Nicaraguan media activists work to fulfil Michael Strangelove's (2015: 223) observation that 'as states renege on their responsibility to provide information systems that promote democratic accountability, the Internet appears well placed to revive the role of local news and an independent and critical press'. For example, Saúl Funez has a YouTube channel to which he uploads the local news reports

[2] Available at https://www.frontlinedefenders.org/en/case/threats-against-lottie-cunningham-wren-and-other-human-rights-defenders.

about the conflicts between Miskitos and *colonos* that are broadcast on Bilwi community television channel TV7. TV7 is also uploading its news reports and documentaries directly to its Facebook page, many of which deal with the conflict in the North Caribbean (and some of which have been produced thanks to international aid agency donations), where they receive thousands of views and are watched by many more viewers than those who see the original television broadcasts.[3] In comparison with mainstream national media coverage, these reports that are produced by indigenous and Creole broadcasters provide more context to the conflict, give extended voice to the Miskito community members that are directly affected, inflect the broader narrative with indigenous 'accents', and ways of knowing and advocate explicitly for indigenous perspectives and positions. What we see is feisty indigenous women and men fighting for their territorial rights with remarkably high levels of both legal and media literacy.

In one such video entitled, 'Conflict between miskitos and *colonos'* (Funez 2015), the voiceover says, 'the Miskitos are tired of being trampled on by the *colonos* in their own home and they are ready to give their lives for Mother Earth. The laws are clear: these lands cannot be confiscated, sold or transferred. Nevertheless, there are corrupt people who are dealing in these transactions and getting rich, the consequences of which must be paid for'. The video cuts to an upset and angry female community member who tells the reporter:

> We are ready to die defending our lands. They came to invade us, and they won't let us go to work. They have killed all the wild animals. Right now there is no peace for the Atlantic Coast. The Atlantic Coast has become a disaster. We don't have the right to live on our own land. This is our own land that our grandparents left to us more than 500 years ago, and they cared for it for their grandchildren, for the next generations. Those that come from the Pacific have no reason to come here.

A male community member then says:

> They [the *colonos*] knew well that these were indigenous lands. From the time of our ancestors, these were indigenous lands. They come and tell us that we are all Nicaraguans. No. Although we are Nicaraguans, you need to realize that Nicaragua has 18 departments and two regions and each department has its own municipalities and its own laws. They created the territories, and now these territories have their own laws in accordance with Law 445, Law 28 and the political constitution of Nicaragua. They made many laws that include us, so the Miskito is also included in those rights.

A second man wearing military fatigues and standing in front of a group of armed Miskitos tells the reporter that eight communities are now engaged in training to defend their lands militarily. The voiceover returns to the reporter, who directly addresses Sandinista denial, neglect and political absence:

> It is up to the government to provide security for its citizens. However, all of the authorities are turning a blind eye and so therefore the conflict between Miskitos and *colonos* continues in the mountains within the territory of Wangki. Therefore, the immediate presence of the police and the army is urgent, to prevent more bloodshed.

[3]See https://www.facebook.com/TV7-RAAN-460905837317274/?fref=nf.

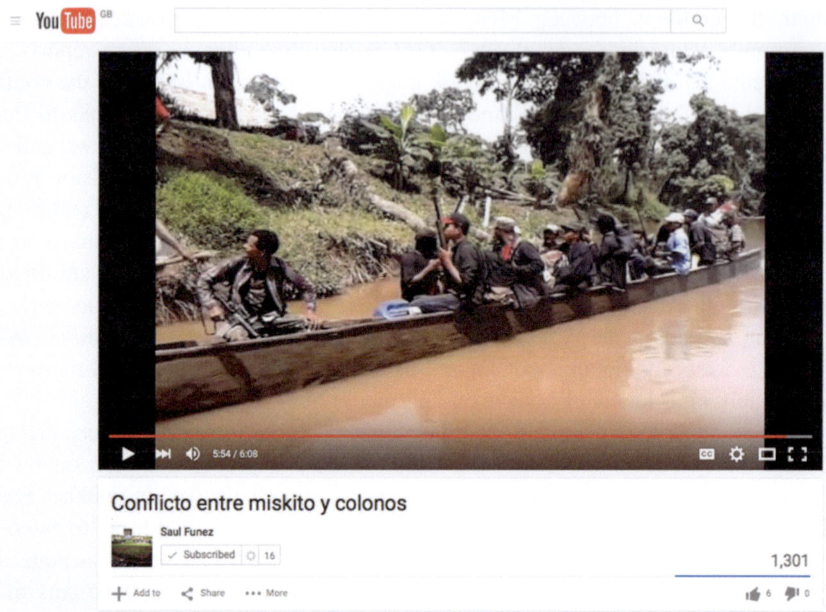

Fig. 4.5 Skiff with armed Miskitos travelling down the Río Coco
Source: Funez 2015

The story closes on an image of a long boat full of armed Miskitos, travelling down the River Coco to confront the *colonos* (see Fig. 4.5), as the absence of state security has forced them to defend themselves and their territories.

The Rama-Kriol community of Bangkukuk Taik in the South Caribbean is facing imminent destruction as a result of the interoceanic canal. Working with a Nicaraguan NGO, the Legal Assistance Centre for Indigenous Peoples (CALPI), the community members have documented the failure of the government to consult with them about the proposed canal and have demonstrated how it would mean the end of their culture and way of life. Their 20-minute YouTube film (Bangkukuk Taik 2015) is analytically rich and contributes to the production and circulation of counter-knowledges that defy and challenge the government's colonial practices, including the interrogation of apparent government lies about why a 'tide marker' was placed in their community, a failure to either inform or consult with the people about the proposed canal, and a promise to deliver development in a form that is incompatible with the survival of Rama culture. But the villagers respond from an alternative epistemology, rooted in a rich history and a self-sufficient economy beyond the state, an anti-capitalist rejection of money and a sense of responsibility instead to land, water, flora and fauna, in which the elders transmit cultural practices and the Rama language to the children, and in which time is understood to be nonlinear, as posterity and future well-being for Rama depends on conserving the efforts of ancestors.[4] The film projects the beauty of everyday life, where food is abundant, culture is vibrant and children are free to swim and play baseball. The sense of place and well-being are palpable. In response to the idea that the canal will bring development, the community pastor, Roberto Wilson says, 'So I told them, I don't need money because we don't live by money. We live by the earth and the water that Jesus gave us in our territory and in our country. I don't need any money. I tell them, money is not good'. The community treasurer, Kathelin Alvarado says, 'In here, we don't buy nothing, we get pretty fresh fish, we plant and we eat *tranquilo*, nobody bothers us'. The communal president of neighbouring community Monkey Point states that Law 840, which establishes the Sandinista government's right to create an interoceanic canal, 'was created with one objective: to make the government could make the project without consulting anyone from Nicaragua. He just take the decision and do it how he wants and do what he wants in the territory. Use the land, the property where he wants to use it without having to consult with no-one'. The communal president's smooth shift of subject from 'the government' to 'he' here signals his rejection of the pretense of Nicaraguan democracy and his recognition and criticism of Ortega's authoritarian *caudillismo*. Similarly, the communal president of Bangkukuk Taik, Carlos Bilis, asserts that 'we don't live by the government, sorry to tell him but we don't live by the government', and aligns the canal project with colonialism in his declaration that the project aims to make the people of his community into the 'slaves' of the *mestizos*. Nevertheless, Bilis defiantly asserts the rights of the Rama community under the law: 'we have the last word about the issue of the canal because the land belongs to the indigenous people'. He occupies then what Enrique Dussel describes as 'the place of affirmation within which the negation in the negation of the system can take place' (quoted in Sáenz 2000: 214).

The Rama-Kriol struggle to defend their community, their culture and their way of life is not anti-modern but rather is a multifrontal struggle for a particular form of indigenous modernity. Indeed, their community pursues this struggle and defends its rights and interests at a variety of scales and in a range of different institutional locations: in the Nicaraguan capital of Managua, at the United Nations, on YouTube and elsewhere on the Internet (including through sites such as Avaaz and IndieGogo), in their interactions with international journalists, and in sites where they conduct detailed research into the canal proposal and develop appropriate forms of legal literacy that are necessary for the defense of their community. They vociferously assert that the canal project, if it goes ahead, will constitute epistemicide and culturecide, as well as the destruction of an ecosystem. The proposal to build a canal in their territory would threaten the Rama-Kriol's 'collective right to survival as an organised people, with control over their habitat as a necessary condition for the reproduction of their culture, for their own development and to carry out their life aspirations', which was established in a 2005 Inter-American

[4]As Silvia Rivera Cusicanqui (2012:96) writes, 'the indigenous world does not conceive of history as linear; the past-future is contained in the present'.

Commission on Human Rights ruling in the case of Ya Kye Axa Indigenous Community v. Paraguay (cited in Lenzerini 2014: 178–179). By positioning the canal as a hypermodern project embedded in modernist development discourses that can only look forward, the film powerfully imagines and asserts an alternative indigenous modernity that struggles against the hegemonic one whose completion relies upon the continued production of coloniality (Mignolo 2005: xv).

In May 2016, facing persistent opposition from the Rama-Kriol, the government deployed a mixture of co-optation and deception to trick some of the community's leaders into signing a document that said they consented to the use of their land for the canal. Pro-Sandinista media reported that the agreement had come after two and a half years of extensive consultation, and that the project is rooted in the indigenous and profoundly anti-capitalist concept of *Buen Vivir*. One article states that co-opted Rama-Kriol president Héctor Thomas Macrae indicated that his people believe 'the canal project will contribute to the *Buen Vivir* of the communities, generate well-being, protect culture, and respect ancestral traditions, and sacred and archaeological sites that are historic patrimony inherited from the ancestors' (Prado Reyes 2016, our translation). At the same time, independent print and broadcast journalists began to circulate alternate narratives, and many Rama-Kriol community members took to the media to denounce the agreement as illegal. On the same day that the pro-Sandinista media announced the agreement, an article in *La Prensa* stated:

> Indigenous and Afro-descendant people from the nine communities that make up the Rama Kriol Territorial Government (GTRK) reported that the signing of an agreement of consent for the use of 263 square kilometres of their territory for the Grand Canal project "is illegal because there has not been a consultation process that conforms to the minimum standards of good faith and those required by national and international law" [Rezaye Álvarez 2016, our translation; see also Vílchez 2016; *Confidencial* 2016].

In addition to issuing press releases to independent media operations, the Rama-Kriol people intensified their use of social media to denounce the agreement, and to confirm that they have not been consulted, nor have they consented to the use of their lands (see Onda Local 2016a, 2016b, 2016c). Thus in July 2016, for example, a new 24-minute Rama-Kriol video challenging the legitimacy of Thomas' claims of communal consent to the canal project was posted on Vimeo and other social media sites (Bangkukuk Taik 2016). The film begins with subtitles that explain the significance of Law 445 (which ensures Rama Creole land rights) and Law 840 (which allows for the construction of the canal), displayed over images of everyday life in the Rama-Kriol communities of the Southern Caribbean Coast of Nicaragua. The video then cuts to a story that was broadcast on Sandinista TV in May 2016, and which reports on the 'historic' agreement between the Rama-Kriol Territorial Government (GTRK) and the Nicaraguan Interoceanic Grand Canal Commission, whereby, according to the report, the GTRK granted the consent of the nine Rama-Kriol communities to the construction of the canal. The remainder of the video travels through these Caribbean communities documenting the refusal of the people to accept the claims for their supposed consent to this agreement, and thus countering the narrative circulated by Sandinista TV. In community after community, people gather to state for the cameras and for the record that they were given no opportunity for free, prior and informed consultation with regard to the proposed canal project and the devastating impacts it would have on their territories. Community members state that they were promised great wealth if they would sign, but refused nevertheless to do so. One community leader explains that 'money never fools me. … Right now, we have a little fish. We have a little lobster. We have a little turtle. Maybe have one animal [per family]. We have a little land. But if that project come here now, we're going to have nothing. We're going to lose everything'. In Bangkukuk Taik, citizens are told that they will be removed from their territory if the canal proceeds, and they protest that the first they've heard of such an outcome is from the makers of the video, despite Sandinista claims that they've been fully informed and have freely consented to the project. In Rama Cay, an impassioned woman proclaims that 'money is temporary, but our territory is for eternity. We have to think, money will be spent, but our territory will always be here, and we have to defend it'. In the video, we see the Rama-Kriol people adding their signatures to a document that announces their rejection of the assertion that they have given their free, prior and informed consent to the canal project. This document will be presented to the International Commission on Human Rights in Washington D.C., as well as to national and international communities via social media.

The Rama-Kriol rejection of neoliberal and neocolonial globalisation and environmentally and culturally destructive development, in tandem with their use of global online media platforms to assert their rights both as Rama and as indigenous peoples, and to connect with international law and global solidarity campaigns, can be understood in terms of what de Sousa Santos (2004: 240, emphasis in original) calls 'the *ecology of trans-scale*', which recovers those elements of the local that are 'not the result of hegemonic globalisation', and which therefore leads toward 'the de-globalisation of the local and its eventual counter-hegemonic re-globalisation'. The visual media activism of Rama-Kriol is one of the ways in which their diverse everyday ecologies are made visible to themselves and the world. These ecologies are pro-environment, pro-children, pro-linguistic protection, and based on a deep sense of place forged through horizontal community logics. Nicholas Mirzoeff (2015: 293) argues that the contemporary expansion of visual activism around the world stems from a widespread sense that '*they* do not represent *us*' (in multiple senses of the term 'represent'). Hence, 'a desire to live otherwise lies behind the worldwide surge in participatory media, from YouTube channels to Snapchatting, and performance' (Mirzoeff, 2015: 295, emphasis added). 'Visual activism' such as that undertaken by Rama-Kriol, and which Mirzoeff (2015: 297) defines as 'the interactions of pixels and actions to make change', is oriented toward the production of 'new ways to see and be seen, and new ways to see the world'.

Costeño-made media differs sharply from Sandinista-controlled media. Even though the anniversary of the autonomy law on 31 October 2015 ended in conflicts between YATAMA and the Sandinistas, and indeed was the day that Juan Herbacio was attacked, the news report on Sandinista-controlled Canal 13 (vivanicaragua13

2015) made no mention of the clashes, did not situate the anniversary in the context of the setbacks to autonomy, and engaged instead in a sexist and exoticizing celebration of ethnic diversity. The piece attributes the achievements of the autonomy process not to the struggles of the Costeños but to the Sandinistas and the Revolution, and points out how the locals 'enjoyed the performance of beautiful young girls [*bellas jovencitas*] who represented all of the municipalities of the South Caribbean in a beauty contest'. It is visual media oriented toward perpetuation of the status quo.

A month after the conflicts in Waspam that revealed the extreme government failure to enforce existing legislation and to provide security to Nicaraguan citizens whose lives are in danger, the government promised to create an interinstitutional commission to formulate the state's response, a promise that never materialized. The Sandinistas did, however, accuse YATAMA deputy and Miskito leader, Brooklyn Rivera, of engaging in illegal land traffic and removed him from office, a move that further enraged many Miskitos who assert that the allegations are false and that the removal of his seat was entirely motivated by politics. Despite the fact that Rivera was removed from office, there was never even any kind of formal investigation of the government's allegations that he had acted illegally.

Media activism on the Coast is not confined to those with the skills or support to make, edit and upload their own films to YouTube. Many Costeños who are perhaps unable to engage in community media or online video production, are nevertheless extremely active on Facebook, where they share material about the conflicts and form solidarities with indigenous groups elsewhere, especially in Panama and Honduras. Facebook pages run by Miskito and Yatama activists involve frequent graphic criticism of the political situation they face (see Fig. 4.6). Rivera's removal from the National Assembly resulted in the further elevation of his status among the Miskito, many of whom posted hastily composed images and memes on Facebook to say so (see Fig. 4.7). The Honduran Miskito Organization MASTA (Miskitu Asla Takanka–Miskitu Indigenous People's Unity) issued a press release on 24 September 2015 in support of Rivera.[5] This release proclaims:

> We have the full confidence and conviction of the innocence of Ta Upla Brooklyn Rivera. We know his trajectory as a leader and we consider him to be someone capable of giving his life for the rights of his people and because of that conviction, he made a personal sacrifice instead of letting his people down.
>
> We deeply regret that a government that should be governing in favour of the most dispossessed, instead engages in fake actions to damage the image of a great leader who for decades has fought and will continue fighting for the good of his people [MASTA 2015, our translation].

[5]Although the Miskito Nation crosses two nation-states, Honduras and Nicaragua, this border has no relevance for most Miskitos. As one Miskito intellectual and mediamaker said to us, 'for us, the indigenous people, there has never been a border. The border is in the mind of governments'.

Fig. 4.6 Graphic Miskito activism on Facebook. The text in the image reads, in English: YATAMA present in the march. No more dictatorship. No more human rights violations. No more imposition. No to the canal. No more manipulations. No more colonization. The Caribbean Coast belongs to the indigenous peoples *Source:* Facebook. Author: Yatama Panama

It is clear that the allegations made against Rivera did not convince many Costeños, who returned him to the National Assembly in the 2016 elections. Furthermore, support for Rivera co-exists with visible criticism on social media of co-opted Costeño politicians. For example, Miskito FSLN politicians such as Raquel Dixon and Carlos Alemán sometimes appear in memes on Facebook, which suggests that alignment with the Nicaraguan power-bloc may be 'a poisoned gift' (Zibechi 2012: 324; see also the discussion regarding Miskito Contra leader Steadman Fagoth in Romero et al. 2015). Memes are ubiquitous in contemporary digital culture and often constitute humorous or satirical takes on political culture. As Limor Shifman (2014: 1518) observes, in contexts that are characterised by high levels of top-down control, 'political memes seem to be more than just a ventilation of anger and frustration; the widespread subversive meme circulation serves as a powerful public display of criticism and distrust. It breaks the facade of optimism and unity presented in official mass media, showing that things are not as "harmonious" as the party would like to present them'. In Nicaragua, while the memes that relate to Daniel Ortega are often humorous, those that circulate about Brooklyn Rivera or Miskito politicians such as Carlos Alemán and Raquel Dixon are often serious, but are widely shared among connected Miskitos in Honduras and Panama as well. Memes are central to convergence culture as they involve the reworking of dominant meanings through the disarticulation and rearticulation of disparate material. They also pose an interesting challenging to the government's attempts to produce ignorance around key issues and events, as memes depend on 'gaps and

Fig. 4.7 Support for Brooklyn Rivera. The text in the image reads, in English: Maximum leader of the indigenous people Brooklyn Rivera. Nightmare of the Sandinista Front *Source:* Facebook. Author: Unknown

inconsistencies' that encourage creators to insert their own meanings (Shifman 2011: 199). Memes thus play a role in the process whereby popular discourses and knowledges participate in 'filling the knowledge vacuums created by official silence', and thus intervening 'into the epistemic void' such silence produces (Glynn 2000: 179).

As the power-bloc intensifies its struggles to exert control while seeking to conceal its activities, grassroots media production, distribution and visibility become key practices of opposition and important modes of countersurveillance (Fiske 1998; also see Thompson 2005; Goldsmith 2010). The use of YouTube and Facebook for decolonial purposes is not, however, straightforward. Both are highly profitable commercial companies that algorithmically track users' viewing preferences and search terms. Yet they are platforms that are 'both industry and user-driven' (Snickars and Vonderau 2009: 11), and can therefore be very useful to grassroots struggles and for 'transmedia mobilization', whereby activists deploy 'any and all available media channels to share their messages' (Jenkins 2016: Kindle Locations 437–438). YouTube is an active node in the convergent media environment where content constantly migrates to and from other parts of the

Internet and other mainstream media. It is routinely viewed on PCs, smartphones, tablets and television sets. Having gained sufficient access to the technological tools and skill sets required to make, edit and upload videos, the challenge for Costeños is to produce videos that are viewed, shared and hopefully acted upon politically. Costeños need 'to be seen and heard' and 'make others hear and see' (Thompson 2005: 49), though this is a potential that won't necessarily be realized. On the other hand, YouTube is also an archive (see for example Gehl 2009), and the YouTube channels created by Costeños, therefore, remain available to those who are not yet but will in the near future be digitally connected. While YouTube as an entity has turned into an 'accidental and disordered public archive' (Burgess and Green 2009: 88), parts of it are becoming quite deliberately curated archives in which human rights abuses can be more systematically documented and accessed.

The significance of these struggles notwithstanding, at the time of this writing the situation in both the North and South Caribbean remained tense and unresolved, especially as a result of the proposed canal and the ongoing conflicts in the North. By 2016, the Sandinista strategy included seeking signatures from indigenous and Creole leaders through underhand, coercive and intimidating means. In both the Rama-Kriol territory and Bluefields, the government continued to ride roughshod over the autonomy law in its pursuit of the canal project. As noted earlier, in Bluefields, the only part of the Caribbean where the demarcation process remains incomplete, the government attempted to persuade community leaders to accept a territory much smaller than that owed to them historically and documented in the earlier stages of the process. At a public meeting on the issue, entry was contingent on signing an 'attendance sheet', which provoked suspicion among Creole leaders. Dolene Miller, a former CONADETI member and Creole leader, denounced this practice in a video that was uploaded to Facebook and shared publicly.[6] In the video, Miller notes how the '*concepto*' or reason for the meeting was left blank. Signing in order to gain entry, as many were required to do, imposed the risk that people would later find their signatures added to a document accepting a much smaller territory than that actually claimed by the community. The extensive comment thread beneath the video captures the divisions on the Caribbean Coast and the levels of co-optation and betrayal that exist there, as well as the magnitude and depth of gratitude to Dolene for taking a stand.

Meanwhile, in the Rama-Kriol community, leaders say they were confused and coerced into signing a document that would permit the construction of the canal across their territory. The GTRK was divided on the matter: six leaders signed and three refused to do so. But afterwards, they told national and international independent media that they had been coerced into signing under quite intimidating conditions, and even those who had signed said they were unsure what it was they had agreed to (see Fendt 2016; Kilpatrick 2016). The meeting was held in the presence of masked police officers and government officials who did not allow them

---

[6]This video can be found here https://www.facebook.com/dolene.miller/videos/vb.100002078737999/945524288860187/?type=2&theater.

to review the document. According to a report in *La Prensa*, it appears that they have signed a document leasing their territory in perpetuity to the Nicaraguan government in exchange for an annual payment of $1 million (Álvarez 2016b). María Luisa Acosta, a lawyer for CALPI, denounced the situation as a violation of human rights, and told *La Prensa* that a perpetual lease is a legal impossibility, as Law 445 permits only temporary leasing and forbids the sale of indigenous lands.

Chapter 5
Mediated Activism in the Pacific

Abstract This chapter focuses on the Pacific region and examines the disruption of Sandinista control over the Nicaraguan mediascape through the interventions of ordinary citizens. It analyzes the mediation of a shooting during an opposition protest in Managua, a protest in the mining community of Mina El Limón, and a march against the interoceanic canal to show how the new media environment complicates the government's efforts to control the meanings that are attached to such events.

Keywords Media convergence · Protest · Twitter · Interoceanic canal
Elections

While the mediated activism surrounding the conflicts on the Caribbean Coast was challenging and disrupting Sandinista strategies for the production of ignorance, media events in the Pacific region, including the national capital of Managua, where the political and cultural context is quite distinct, began to have similar repercussions. Every Wednesday, up until the November 2016 elections, a group supporting the opposition parties MRS and PLI, along with other civil society activists, held a peaceful protest outside the Supreme Electoral Council in Managua to call for clean elections. These peaceful protesters became used to the heavy deployments of riot police that greeted their presence in the square each week. During the protest of 2 September 2015, someone fired four shots with a pistol. These shots were fired just a few metres from a large group of riot police and Juan Valle Valle, the chief of Managua's traffic patrol. Despite the fact that the shooter endangered many lives by firing in a public place, the police present that day said they had seen nothing. They apparently hoped their denials would put the matter to bed and allow the shooting to do its work of deterring popular participation in future protests. Those in power did not, however, consider the realities of the new media environment. A number of people at the protest had used their cell phones to film and photograph the incident. Many of them shared photos of the shooter on Twitter and Facebook and uploaded films of the incident to YouTube (see *Confidencial* 2015). Within hours, the shooter had been identified as Samir Matamoros.

J. Cupples and K. Glynn, *Shifting Nicaraguan Mediascapes*,
SpringerBriefs in Latin American Studies,
https://doi.org/10.1007/978-3-319-64319-9_5

Fig. 5.1 Samir Matamoros. Image of Samir Matamoros in *Confidencial.* Author: Mario López Photograph reproduced with permission of *Confidencial*

The social media activity that led to the rapid identification of Matamoros spread quickly to the independent media, which also began to circulate the shooter's image (see Figs. 5.1 and 5.2), thus leaving the police with no choice but to arrest him. The police held a press conference on the day after the shooting (albeit one at which the press was forbidden from asking questions), during which they identified Matamoros as a 'common delinquent'. By Friday, *Confidencial* had revealed that Matamoros was a former gang member who was receiving support from the Centre for the Prevention of Violence (CEPREV), an NGO led by Sandinista dissident, Mónica Zalaquett,that encourages young people to abandon violent gangs. *Confidencial* also reported that in 2014, Matamoros had been recruited by the Sandinista Youth. After the publication of *Confidencial*'s report, Daniel Ortega inappropriately intervened in the judicial process by defending Matamoros' actions and stating that the shooter 'didn't injure anyone with his shots', and that 'it is clear that he did not shoot to kill' (Romero 2015c). Ortega's intervention amply revealed the levels of collusion in Nicaragua between the executive, the judiciary and the police, and was criticized by a number of human rights organizations. At his judicial hearing, which no independent media were allowed to attend, Matamoros 'confessed' that he had been persuaded to fire his gun by Mónica Zalaquett, and was sentenced to four years and 30 days imprisonment (*La Prensa* 2015c). Pro-FSLN media responded by claiming that CEPREV was 'linked to right-wing

Fig. 5.2 Samir Matamoros. Image of Samir Matamoros in *La Prensa.* Author: J Torres Photograph reproduced with permission of *La Prensa*

organizations with whom they plan criminal actions in an attempt to destabilize the country' (Álvarez 2015).

These events unleashed a wave of criticism against the government and its allies that reveal their vulnerability to popular mobilization in the face of FSLN attempts to exert control over the media discourses and narratives that secure their power. For example, Mirando Aburto (2015, our translation) used the occasion to draw attention to 'the role played by the *Orteguista* shock forces, which have brutally disrupted so many protests', and to indict the Sandinistas' efforts to discredit their political opponent, Mónica Zalaquett. Nicaraguan social media similarly exploded with expressions of outrage over the government's blundering efforts to smear Zalaquett, and the Twitter hashtags #YoEstoyconMonica (#IamwithMonica) and #apoyomonicazalaquettceprev (#Isupportmonicazalaquettceprev) quickly began trending. The Catholic Church responded too; both Silvio Báez, the auxiliary bishop of Managua, and Cardinal Leopoldo Brenes criticized the government for its 'un-Christian' treatment of Zalaquett (*Nicaragua Hoy* 2015). Famed Nicaraguan poet and novelist, Gioconda Belli (2015), wrote about the important work being done by Zalaquett and CEPREV, who were actively raising awareness of how dominant expressions of masculinity lead to violence, and helping hundreds of young people from Managua's urban neighbourhoods find a different path. By stark contrast, Belli observed, the government was actively recruiting young people and sending them to conduct attacks on peaceful opposition protests.

Former Sandinista *comandante* and MRS leader Dora María Téllez sees the Matamoros incident as the unmasking of Ortega. In an article entitled 'Ortega without his balaclava' (*Ortega sin pasamontañas*), Téllez (2015, our translation) writes that the recruitment of gang members to attack opposition protests

> is not a new strategy. It's been in place since 2008. (…) It is the modus operandus of the Ortega family: they speak of love and send others to carry out criminal acts, to claim that their hands are clean. What is new now is that Ortega has been completely unmasked. In less than 24 hours, we all learned that Samir Matamoros is a member of the *grupos de choque* of Orteguismo. The shooter and the motocyclist who gave him a ride away from the place were identified on social media and by participants in the Wednesday protest. (…) The complicity of the police at the highest level was in plain sight, when they did absolutely nothing. But it was all photographed, videoed and it has been seen by thousands of Nicaraguans. (…) The accusation against Mónica Zalaquett is just the smoke screen that Ortega and the police chiefs need. It is like the trick the magicians use to get the audience to look the other way, while they rearrange the stage. Only, on this occasion, it has failed. It was all too clumsy and Ortega's unmasking has been seen and is being seen by everyone.

These criticisms of covert Sandinista strategy spread rapidly due to the dynamics of media convergence: as images and videos of Matamoros circulated virally across platforms, the event became one that even the pro-government media could not ignore. A combination of expanded popular access to digital media production tools and the increased speed of media circulation thus mean that established media organizations cannot afford to opt out of the process, but rather must struggle harder than ever to try to keep up with their new, grassroots competitors. In the age of what Jenkins et al. (2013) call 'spreadable media', 'what happened in a predigital world now occurs with exponentially greater speed and scope' (p. 12), and 'the top-down hierarchies of the broadcast era now coexist with the integrated system of participatory channels' (p. 17). Consequently, the official media can no longer choose merely to remain silent, however, much it may suit their interests to do so. The combination of enhanced media circulatory speed and expanded popular participation thus effectively thwarted the Sandinista government's attempts to control the Matamoros narrative, a failure that was to continue in the coming weeks as further media events erupted and their meanings were subjected to popular discursive contestation.

Mina El Limón is a gold mining community in León. Over the past decades, the miners there have frequently mobilized for better working conditions. The gold mine has a long history, but was nationalized during the revolution and privatized through a series of concession regimes after 1990. The current concessionaire is a Canadian multinational named B2Gold, which employs 800 miners and supplies the community's electricity. In May 2015, there were serious protests after the company started cutting off the electricity from 8 am until 8 pm (López 2015). In October 2015, tensions escalated when B2Gold fired three trade union leaders, and the police detained one of them, a move that gave rise to a strike and a wave of protests, as the community

Fig. 5.3 Confrontation in Mina El Limón. *Source* Confidencial Photograph reproduced with permission of *Confidencial*

demanded that the three sacked workers be reinstated. The ostensibly 'socialist' government of Daniel Ortega sided with the foreign multinational company rather than with the sacked trade unionists and sent in the riot police. This led to violent confrontations between miners and cops, and resulted in the death of an officer and injuries to more than 30 people, the majority of whom were members of the police force. In response, security forces placed the community under siege, cutting off its water supply and preventing delivery of inbound food. The women of the community dressed themselves in black and continued to protest in the days that followed, chanting 'Daniel Ortega died in Mina El Limón' (Torres and López 2015). As with the Matamoros affair, the government tried to minimise awareness of the incident by keeping both independent media and human rights organizations out of the community, and announcing that the situation was under control (see *El 19 Digital* 2015; González J 2015). Despite these attempts to keep the events of Mina El Limón out of the media, horrific images of confrontations between the women protesting and riot police began to circulate in independent media and through social media (see Fig. 5.3). For example, Nicaraguan human rights organisation CENIDH took to Twitter to denounce the government for preventing CENIDH from doing its work, and to contest the assertions being promoted through Sandinista media that peace had been restored to Mina El Limón.[1]

[1]For instance, on 18 October 2015, CENIDH sent out the following two tweets:

Pro-Sandinista media shifted their focus from the uprising in Mina El Limón to an upcoming boxing match between Nicaraguan Román 'Chocolatito' González and Brian Veloria, scheduled for 17 October in New York. Nicaraguans are fanatical about boxing, and the government had provided substantial financial support for González, *El Chocolatito*, and would be broadcasting the fight on free-to-air Sandinista television. Social media participants from the popular sectors, however, responded to the Sandinistas' attempt to articulate Mina El Limón to discourses of the restoration of peace by instead linking the mining community to images and discourses of agonistic struggle associated with the upcoming boxing match. Hence, for instance, Nicaraguan Twitter users added photos of violence in Mina El Limón to the hashtags #ChocolatitoOrgullodemipais (#Chocolatitoprideofmycountry) and #Vamoschocolatito (#Let'sgochocolatito). B2Gold then retaliated by cutting off the electricity supply to prevent the residents of Mina El Limón from watching the boxing match on television. A reading of tweets from 17-20 October 2015 concerning Mina El Limón shows that while those stemming from Sandinista-linked sources stress claims that peace and calm have been restored to the community, a much larger deluge of microblogged messages emphasise the continuation of state-led violence, confrontations, militarization and a state of siege in the mining community. There are then two competing narratives at work that can be consumed side by side and assessed accordingly. This instance almost literalizes growing claims about the contemporary media environment as an imagistic battleground and a multitiered public sphere (see Dayan 2009). While the power-bloc may assert that peace and order have been restored, such claims are swamped by a flood of tweets that depict the situation in very different terms.

Nor was social movement mobilization confined to the uprising in Mina El Limón, which occured at the same time as anti-canal activists were organising a protest march against the *Orteguista* megaproject. This march was scheduled to take place on 27 October 2015, just ten days after the siege of Mina El Limón. Once again, government forces did everything in their power to prevent the protest. For instance, they organised a countermarch, dubbed the 'Great Walk for Work and Peace, United Nicaragua Triumphs', which was scheduled for the same day as the anti-canal protest and was to include state employees, high school students and members of the Sandinista Youth, who would tie-up the entire urban bus fleet of Managua and thus deprive non-participants of access to public transportation for the day. They also used El Chocolatito, the Nicaraguan boxer, to promote the countermarch (see Chávez 2015), and tried to prevent *campesinos* who live in areas located in the proposed canal's path from reaching the anti-canal march by disabling public transportation. So, many of these *campesinos* arranged to travel

1. 'they are preventing us from doing our job. Comm Cuadra said "I have orders from above not to let in the media nor you people from cenidh"' ('*impiden realizar nuestra labour. Com Cuadra dijo "tengo ordenes superior de no dejar pasar los medios de comunicación ni ustedes del cenidh*"').

2. 'Inhabitants refute the news item from canal 4, it is not true that calm returned, the village of Mina is militarized' ('*Pobladores desmienten noticia del canal 4, no es cierto q volvio la calma lo q hay es un estado de sitio, pueblo dela Mina esta militarizado*').

alternatively on foot or in cattle trucks, only to be confronted upon their arrival in Managua by riot police, *grupos de choque*, and counter-protestors. Despite such obstacles, many *campesinos* living in the path of the proposed canal were joined by thousands of others in a spectacular display of opposition. Some who made it as far as Managua were prevented by police blockades from reaching the National Assembly, while others broke through these blockades and continued onward. The headline in *La Prensa* the next day was, 'Orteguismo did everything but was unable [to stop the march]' (Romero et al. 2015). The marchers linked their opposition to the canal to many other significant political issues, such as women's and indigenous rights.

On the day of the anti-canal march, Nicaraguan social media was bursting with activity. Many were celebrating and sharing the success of the march and clearly articulating how the canal threatened *campesino* and indigenous land rights, Nicaragua's sovereignty and the Lake Nicaragua ecosystem. One activist uploaded a filmed interview with a member of the Sandinista Youth who had participated in the government's countermarch, and yet who could scarcely explain what he was marching for. This interview was posted to a Facebook page called 'Trolling Daniel Ortega' ('*Trolleando a Daniel Ortega*' 2015), a popular, critical and satirical site where ordinary Nicaraguans have made a media space to mock and speak out against their increasingly authoritarian president. When he was asked why he joined the countermarch, the young Sandinista supporter from El Coral, Chontales, who was one of 70 or 80 transported some 230 kilometres by the government for the event, replied that 'we are participating in this activity to recognize that our *comandante*, Daniel Ortega, our leader, our main leader of our country … it is to show in this walk all of the support that he is giving us with our work or studies, rectifying the dignity that we deserve'. Another video showed a short speech given by the boxer, *El Chocolatito*, at a Sandinista rally held at the end of the countermarch. In his speech, El Chocolatito proclaims, 'Long live the youth. Long live *Comandante* Daniel Ortega. We are heading for more victories. Long live the *comandante*. We are heading for more work and we are heading for more victories' (Chamorro and Castillo 2015). The recontextualisation of such empty political rhetoric from the Sandinista countermarch and rally to a satirical and critical Facebook page serves to undermine the power of such rhetoric in Sandinista strategies for the production of complacency and ignorance.

Many Nicaraguans are using social media in such ways to draw attention to the disparities between Sandinista rhetoric and the lived social realities of their everyday lives. One widely viewed (60,000 times) and shared (3,000 times) online video is striking in this regard. In this video, images of Sandinista repression are accompanied by the party's 2006 election campaign theme, a Spanish language and reggaeton remix of John Lennon's 'Give Peace a Chance'. The video begins with the face and words of Daniel Ortega professing to be an agent of peace, progress, happiness and expanded possibility in Nicaragua, then cuts to repeated images of police brutality as the theme tune plays on (Marlon Moreno 2015). This example helps illustrate the 'erosion' of the 'cultural authority' of traditional media that has occurred 'under the conditions of post-television culture', such that 'the online audience will produce a counter-discourse' when official sources are found to be wanting. In this way, 'amateur videographers are becoming an agenda-setting force which represents a challenge to traditional news sources' (Strangelove 2015: 221).

The juxtaposition of *Orteguista* rhetoric with contrapuntal images and discourses as a strategy for criticising the contemporary state of official *Sandinismo* is not confined to Nicaraguan media sites. In one episode of *Bayly*, for instance, which airs on the Miami-based broadcast network Mega TV, satirical Peruvian host Jaime Bayly plays a clip of Daniel Ortega declaiming against anti-imperialism, to which Bayly responds, 'What an idiot' ('*Qué pedazo de idiota*') (Nole Importa 2012).[2] Bayly then goes on to talk of Daniel Ortega's stepdaughter, Zoilamérica Narvaéz, who in 1998 accused Ortega of raping her repeatedly for years, beginning when she was 11, an allegation she maintains to this day (see Cupples 2002). Bayly asserts that if Nicaragua were a civilized country, Daniel Ortega would be in jail. In 2015, as Sandinista authoritarianism and repression were increasing, Carlos Fernando Chamorro, the host of the weekly Nicaraguan current affairs show, *Esta Semana*, was interviewed by Jorge Ramos on Univisión, a US TV network that enjoys the largest Spanish-speaking audience in the world. Ramos and Chamorro discuss the control exerted and extraordinary economic wealth held by Daniel Ortega, his wife and his family (*Univisión Noticias* 2015). This interview was broadcast nationally in the United States and internationally through YouTube, and was widely shared through other social media platforms.

Just as Nicaraguans' bottom-up media circulation is beyond the control of Daniel Ortega despite his family's vast media holdings, neither can he constrain foreign and pan-Latin American media, much of which draws attention to FSLN corruption and authoritarianism. The risk to the party of attempting to wrap a positive Sandinista narrative around the figure of Daniel Ortega, while engaging in a strategic politics of not knowing, is that in the age of media convergence, such a strategy makes Ortega particularly prone to scandal politics and to other forms of contestation associated with the widespread circulation of counterdiscourses linked to the 'rise of mediated visibility' (Thompson 2005: 35; also see Castells 2007). For instance, around the time of the canal march, some foreign media began to report allegations that Ortega had fathered a child with a 15-year-old girl, and on 22 October 2015, the Miami-based *Diario de las Américas* ran a story with the headline 'My daughter was raped by Daniel Ortega'. The article claims that Ortega's personal assistant made several bank deposits to the alleged victim's brother, who is now in jail in Managua after he denounced the president (Flores 2015). This story was widely shared and commented on by Nicaraguans on social media, as was a 17 minute story from the 8 October edition of a current affairs show, *A Mano Limpia* on *América TeVé*, also based in Florida, examining the older

[2]Daniel Ortega says of the US government that 'it presents itself as the most exemplary democracy in the world, when in reality it is the most enormous and most striking tyranny and dictatorship that has existed in all of humanity' (Nole Importa 2012).

child sexual abuse allegations and including an interview with Ortega's step-daughter, Zoilamérica (*A Mano Limpia* 2015). On the one hand, such US-originated stories resonate with well-worn discourses and images of the Western popular 'folk devil' of the Latin American communist dictator (Manzano 2014: 113) and thus are potentially motivated by and serve the interests of specific right-wing agents and agendas. On the other hand, however, what is particularly interesting here is the way in which the contemporary, convergent media environment enables such stories to be recontextualised and thus repurposed for democratic struggles engaged by progressive Nicaraguans. Hence, while the independent Nicaraguan media steered completely clear of this story, it was nevertheless widely circulated through the social media accounts of many Nicaraguans who are struggling to advance democratic aims.

Furthermore, these examples illustrate the ways in which struggles over the Nicaraguan government's strategies for the production of ignorance are extended from a national to a global terrain in the contemporary media environment, as the FSLN faces growing calls for accountability and political action by international organizations. For instance, when the Special Rapporteur of the United Nations issued a joint allegation letter on 23 February 2015 expressing concern about the Nicaraguan government's deployment of the excessive use of force and arbitrary detention targeting peaceful protesters against the interoceanic canal proposal, the Nicaraguan government simply refused to respond (United Nations Special Rapporteur 2015). Similarly, the government, and specifically Rosario Murillo, has simply ignored repeated requests for interviews by Univisión journalist Mario Vallejo after a Cuban refugee crisis broke out on the Nicaraguan-Costa Rican border. Vallejo responded by publicly posting his unanswered requests to his Facebook page, which has subsequently been 'liked' extensively and circulated widely.[3]

In the months leading up to the 2016 presidential elections, Daniel Ortega and the FSLN-aligned institutions enacted a number of measures designed to eliminate the possibility of any viable electoral challenge from the opposition. The Nicaraguan government also deported several foreign environmental activists and a US academic, Evan Ellis, who had come to research the interoceanic canal (AP 2016a; Lakhani 2016). They also briefly arrested and then freed anti-canal *campesina* leader Francisca Ramírez (González A 2016) and feminist activist Patricia Orozco (Romero 2016b). Ortega also announced in June that there would be no election observers, an illegal move in light of the fact that international observation is enshrined in Nicaraguan electoral law. The Sandinista-controlled Supreme Court of Justice then proceeded to eliminate Ortega's chief electoral competitors, Luis Callejas and Violeta Granera, who had only days earlier been announced as candidates by the newly formed Coalition for Democracy. The Coalition for Democracy was spearheaded by Eduardo Montealegre, leader of the PLI, with the support of the MRS. The Supreme Court of Justice first removed Montealegre from

[3]This page is available here: https://www.facebook.com/mvallejotv/posts/1725368464349367.

the leadership of the PRI and replaced him with Pedro Reyes, who was widely seen as an FSLN puppet and who was therefore unacceptable to PLI deputies (Álvarez and Chamorro 2016). The Supreme Court then annulled the candidacies of Callejas and Granera, and thus left the electoral field wide open for Ortega. At that point, Reyes announced that he would run as the PLI's candidate for the presidency. Shortly thereafter, however, Reyes withdrew from the contest on the basis that he had inadequate time to mount an effective challenge to Ortega (Chamorro Mendieta 2016).

At the end of July, 28 opposition deputies from the PLI and MRS were removed from office for their lack of obedience to Reyes, an action that was condemned by large numbers of human rights organizations in the Americas, including the Washington Office on Latin America (WOLA) and the Inter-American Platform of Human Rights, Democracy and Development (PIDHDD).[4] A week later, Ortega named his wife, Rosario Murillo, as his presidential running mate. As Ortega's efforts to further consolidate his grip on power intensified, so too did the circulation of counterdiscourses through the convergent media environment. After the nepotistic nomination of Murillo for vice-president, Nicaraguan social media exploded so furiously that it became impossible to keep up with the volume of critical activity online. Additionally, mainstream international media began to take a renewed interest in Nicaragua. In early August 2016, many articles discussed the ways in which Daniel Ortega was threatening Nicaraguan democracy, eliminating political pluralism and turning the upcoming elections into a farcical affair that would have no credibility (see for example AP 2016b; Jones 2016; Reuters 2016; Salinas 2016; *Semana* 2016). The 2016 elections thus took place without the usual electoral fervour that characterised the elections of 2001, 2006 and 2011 (see Cupples and Larios 2005; Cupples 2009), and with very little evidence of active campaigning by any of the parties on the ballot apart from Ortega. One commentator opined that Nicaragua was 'living through one of the most tragic and dark periods of its history since the end of the regime of terror imposed by Anastasio Somoza' (Mosquera 2016, our translation). In an interview with the Mexican newspaper *Milenio*, ousted MRS deputy Victor Hugo Tinoco described the situation in similar terms, remarking that Nicaragua was 'experiencing the most serious institutional setback and dismantling of democracy since the end of the war' in 1990 (Contreras 2016, our translation).

In the transnational convergent media environment, such oppositional discourses of de-democratization flow readily across media forms, spaces, technologies and platforms. For example, Murillo's nomination by her husband featured in both late-night US TV comedy and the opening ceremony of the Olympic Games in Rio. James Cordon, host of CBS' *The Late Late Show with James Corden* mocked the decision and ridiculed Ortega and Murillo. Corden recontextualised the story and resignified Sandinista authoritarianism in terms of the quotidian politics and

[4]For a complete list of human rights organizations that condemned the FSLN's actions, see CENIDH (2016).

tensions of marital relations ('No honey, I told *you* to put down the rebels'. 'Great! So nobody put down the rebels. Well I hope you like rebels!') (*The Late Late Show with James Corden* 2016). This satirical piece was widely covered in newspapers and journalistic websites across Latin America; within three days it had been viewed on YouTube almost 150,000 times. When Nicaragua's five athletes appeared before the crowd during the opening ceremony of the Rio Olympics, BBC commentator Hazel Irvine likened Ortega's nomination of Murillo to the behaviour of the fictitious, murderous, Machiavellian and megalomaniacal US president from the Netflix drama series *House of Cards* and announced, 'Frank Underwood eat your heart out!'[5]

By eliminating his political opponents, Ortega created the conditions for electoral victory but severely eroded the credibility and legitimacy upon which hegemony in some measure necessarily depends. The struggle of the Costeños against settler violence continues, as does the oppositional movement against the proposed canal. Indeed, the strength of this movement was recognized by *Forbes* magazine in 2016 when it designated the anti-canal leader, Francisca Ramírez, as the 44th most powerful woman in Central America, in a list that included former presidents and bankers (Cordero 2016). The FSLN's molar strategy for the production of ignorance and the consolidation of power is challenged by this anti-canal movement, by the dispersed and spontaneous tactics of Nicaraguan media activists, and by other forms of transnational and pan-Latin Americanized media. By March 2017, *Confidencial* reported that HKND's presence in Nicaragua was waning, that there was still no evidence of canal construction, and that Wang Jing had disappeared from the country; consequently, it was possible to speculate that the *Orteguista* megaproject was in doubt (*Confidencial* 2017). But as Law 840 has not been repealed, *campesinos* in threatened areas continue to mobilize. Hence there are diverse modes of media convergence at work that transect one another and produce unexpected alliances and new topological configurations and political potentials.

[5]In season 4 of the series, Underwood names his wife Carrie as his running mate.

Chapter 6
Ignorance and Illegibility

Abstract The final chapter assesses the current conjuncture as one in which both democracy and authoritarianism are under threat. It returns to questions surrounding the government's attempts to produce public ignorance and illegibility, and examines grassroots media interventions that exploit gaps and absences that are themselves created by the Sandinista's own strategic efforts. These popular interventions mobilize counter-discourses and counter-knowledges that rearticulate official modes of sensemaking and thus help to maintain the conditions of possibility for decoloniality and democratization.

Keywords Democratization · Authoritarianism · Ignorance · Illegibility Decoloniality

The current conjuncture in Nicaragua is one in which both democracy and authoritarianism are under threat. As with all conjunctural crises, there is no way of knowing how or when this crisis will be resolved (Hall et al. 2013: xv). It is complicated in part because we are dealing with competing regimes of knowledge and multiple modalities of power. Ortega's strategy is a highly calculated one based on control of both space and resources. It aims to repress challenges to his leadership and longevity in power, and to prevent the full autonomy of the Caribbean Coast, which would put in question the territorial integrity and *mestizo* ideology upon which the Nicaraguan state is based, as are too, therefore, the highly profitable forms of capital accumulation enjoyed by the power-bloc, and the consequent, continued dispossession of the poor Nicaraguan majority. The Sandinista-led power-bloc exerts control through a combination of secrecy, overt repression, aggressive displays of coercive state force and a politics of not-knowing whereby hegemonic social formations seek to 'destroy non-hegemonic and potentially counter-hegemonic social experience' (de Sousa Santos 2004: 238), including the uncomfortable truths, alternative knowledges and existing problems generated by such experience. The problem that such hegemonic strategies for the production of ignorance must confront is that the experiences of the subordinated give rise to the continuous generation of counter-discourses and counter-knowledges capable of

J. Cupples and K. Glynn, *Shifting Nicaraguan Mediascapes*,
SpringerBriefs in Latin American Studies,
https://doi.org/10.1007/978-3-319-64319-9_6

reasserting that which the power-bloc would render effectively non-existent or, to put it differently, that whose existence the power-bloc seeks to render ineffective. The everyday experiences of most Nicaraguans, for example, continuously present them with reasons to discount and contest the claim that Nicaragua is 'heading for more victories'. And contest it they do.

The behaviour of the Sandinista government often appears to be highly arbitrary, irrational and open to ridicule and satirisation. Moreover, its actions are replete with repressive tactics, extreme secrecy, a self-serving disregard for the rule of law and an apparent desire to foment environmental disaster. It is useful here to consider the work of Linsey McGoey (2007) and Veena Das (2004), which demonstrates how ignorance and illegibility can be deployed as strategic weapons. McGoey draws on Nietzschian and Foucauldian notions of a will-to-ignorance, and suggests that feigning ignorance can be a useful anti-strategy in contemporary bureaucracies that are faced with demands for transparency and procedural justice. Bureaucratic ignorance can thus be presented as an aberrant deviation from 'correct procedure rather than endemic to the system itself', despite the fact that such ignorance enables bureaucracies to exert control over 'the very information' they have an 'interest in concealing' (McGoey 2007: 217–8). In the Nicaraguan context, such anti-strategies of bureaucratic ignorance are systemically concealed within an ongoing barrage of official, happy (non)communication. Similarly, Das (2004: 245) draws on fieldwork in India to ask how a state can 'claim legitimacy in the face of obvious forgeries' and 'corruption within its own procedures'. She argues that 'bureaucratic logic displaces notions of irrationality and panic' onto the public itself, and thereby claims 'rationality' for its own bureaucratized and deliberate avoidance of transparency. In other words, it is through the deliberate modulation of illegibility and irrationality that the state attempts to produce its own legitimacy. In Nicaragua, the government proliferates illegibilities and irrationalities, which it seeks to mask with spectacles of happiness, metallic trees and stage-managed, pro-government marches and rallies. The irony is that such spectacles appear to many of Nicaragua's subordinated populations as so many absurdities in their own right.

By the same token, Das observes that hegemonic attempts at the modulation of illegibility and irrationality can only ever succeed up to a point, for illegibility and irrationality produce inevitable gaps and absences in which the subordinated and excluded can 'insert themselves' and struggle to produce 'new modalities of rule' (p. 249). Increasingly, the spaces of ignorance and absence created within and through FSLN discourses are being filled by popular counter-discourses and counter-knowledges that rearticulate official modes of sensemaking and thus intensify the conjunctural crisis that afflicts the Nicaraguan state. Because these popular counter-discourses and counter-knowledges emerge from a failure of recognition, are socially dispersed, and mobilize decolonizing modes of exteriority that evade monocultural hegemonic logics, they often appear illegible from the perspectives of the state. The social movements that the Nicaraguan state seeks to discipline do not control an army, police force, or national budget, and might even find themselves deprived of government handouts if they express opposition openly. As Zibechi (2012: 259) notes, 'the dominated do not act symmetrically in relation to those dominating them and, for that reason, do not formulate a rational programme that they set out to implement'. But Miskito and Creole people have an advantage that *mestizo* elites lack: they are used to negotiating Eurocentric and *mestizo* knowledges, and have a long history of living between worlds (or *entremundos*; see Mignolo 2005; Escobar 2007).

As Stuart Hall et al. (2013: xii) argue, hegemonic blocs depend on the cultural power 'to signify and thus give events a social meaning, and to win society to "their definition of the situation"'. The government's need to step-up its attempts to silence radio shows and threaten journalists suggests the failure of Sandinista discourses to resonate effectively with the knowledges and experiences generated from other positions within the social formation. The mobilization of government forces in acts of state-sanctioned violence against indigenous, Black Creole and dissident populations thus signals a shift in hegemonic strategy along the Gramscian continuum of power that runs from the establishment of consent to coercion. Consequently, riot forces are deployed more and more routinely under the guise of ordinary policing, Miskito leaders are accused of fictitious crimes, and journalists are threatened, all while positive narratives about the state of the nation circulate across Sandinista-owned media platforms. But if the Sandinista definitions of situations and events increasingly fail to resonate with the everyday experiences of ordinary people and provide no scope for alternative ways of knowing, their authority is likely to come under increasing pressure, and the social formation to continue to fracture. As Castells (2007: 238) argues, 'while coercion and fear are critical sources for imposing the will of the dominants over the dominated, few institutional systems can last long if they are predominantly based on sheer repression. Torturing bodies is less effective than shaping minds'.

As William Rowe and Vivian Shelling (1991) warned us more than two decades ago, it is important not to assume that the popular cultures of subordinated peoples contain subversive and democratising resources adequate to the production of grassroots political transformation. But it is just as important to recognize that there are alternative cultural practices and knowledges that have survived against the odds in Nicaragua, and there is some evidence to suggest that the forms of democratized media access available in the new media environment are helping give rise to the appearance of new sites for the rearticulation and recirculation of such knowledges, and for the pursuit of transformative political and cultural agendas (although, as we have noted, such pursuits are not without risks). Intertextual interactions between disparate media discourses, genres, formats, platforms and technologies unpredictably connect distinct political issues and can raise awareness of potential intersections between struggles for black and indigenous rights, women's rights, *mestizo campesino* rights and environmental protection. The knowledges put into circulation through the media practices of black and indigenous Nicaraguans in the face of coloniality, repression and bureaucratic strategies for the production of ignorance are, like other popular cultural forms, 'composed of antagonisms and unstable elements' (Hall 2006 [1981]: 484). We can see how Costeño knowledges combine Miskito and Creole cosmovisions with anti-capitalist and anti-communist discourses, and with essentialist and anti-essentialist anti-racisms. They also draw strategically on European notions of law and citizenship, albeit in indigenised and hybridized ways, and sometimes reproduce (albeit perhaps strategically, ironically and knowingly) Western environmentalist fantasies of indigenous peoples as saviours of nature.[1] Costeños both assert their rights as Nicaraguans and construct Nicaragua as a foreign territory beyond the Mosquitia that is inhabited not by *mestizos* but by Spaniards.[2] Sometimes, they even look back nostalgically on the Somoza dictatorship, or fight for indigenous and Afro-descendant rights while expressing homophobic attitudes towards gays and lesbians. While their land titling and demarcation strategies involve the translation of indigenous knowledges into forms that align with Western cartographic conventions that are thus legible to state elites (Nietschmann 1995; Finley-Brook and Offen 2009; Mollett 2013), such acts of strategic epistemological rearticulation do nothing to resolve or wipe away the apparent lack of political coherence we've noted here.[3]

The apparent lack of coherence that may be ascribed to Costeño discourses and knowledges might be understood to carry a political advantage, as it produces an illegibility of its own that makes it difficult for the Sandinista power-bloc to exert effective control over them. As Laura Kipnis (1992: 387) has suggested in another context, if Costeño discourses seem 'politically incoherent' from the standpoint of 'traditional political alliances and political oppositions', it is because of the ways in which Costeño knowledges put such traditional alliances and oppositions in question. The ways in which Costeños are blurring and moving beyond the left versus right political binary is perhaps evidence of a decolonial politics at work. After all, as Ramón Grosfoguel (2012) writes, the Westernized left in Latin America thinks from the same Christian-centric cosmology as the right and reproduces the same modes of epistemic racism and sexism. Reflecting on political processes in contemporary Bolivia, Arturo Escobar (2010) sees the emergence of a third political space, a decolonial one, that is not ideologically aligned with the Westernized left or right and that is productive of alternative imaginations. While YATAMA participates in the Nicaraguan political system in ways that may appear similar to the participation of political parties in Europe, it is not an ideological right- or left-wing party, and it creates a space in which Miskito cosmovisions are vocalized and respected, and indigenous modes of governance are kept alive. Indeed, these heterogeneous discursive sites constitute what Enrique Dussel (1977) would call alterity, in the sense that Costeños are thinking and speaking

[1]In one of their YouTube videos, CEJUDHCAN (2015a) interviews Costeño participants in front of a banner that reads, 'We indigenous/Afro-descendant peoples live in harmony with nature'.

[2]Costeños still frequently refer to Pacific Nicaraguans as 'Spaniards'.

[3]In the Honduran part of the Mosquitia, such legibility depends on Miskito and Garifuna communities clarifying overlapping claims and jointly managed spaces. Sharlene Mollett's (2013) work on the fraught complexities of land titling there demonstrates that legibility is not in and of itself enough to guarantee rights (p. 1234). As in Nicaragua, the Honduran Miskito population is also struggling with the presence of *colonos*.

from positions of *relative* or *partial* exteriority. As Grosfoguel (2015), following Dussel argues, there are alternative epistemologies that have survived Eurocentric modernity, albeit in impure and hybridized forms. These epistemologies can be understood as resources for decolonial and transmodern projects. Thus, subalternised populations can take concepts such as *democracy* and *human rights*, which have been 'kidnapped' by the West, and 'decolonize them in different directions' (Grosfoguel 2015: 41). The repeated use of legal language such as the text and terminology of Law 445 in everyday discourse, in combination with pluriversal narratives in diverse online and offline spaces, is evidence of an ongoing struggle for the construction of a transmodern decoloniality.

References

Acosta M L (2014) El canal y los pueblos indígenas. *Confidencial* 12 October http://www.confidencial.com.ni/archivos/articulo/19683/el-canal-y-los-pueblos-indigenas (Accessed 21 November).

Acosta M L (2015) El impacto de la ley del gran canal interocéanico de Nicaragua sobre los pueblos indígenas y afrodescendientes de Nicaragua. *Cuaderno Jurídico y Político* 1(2): 21–31.

Adams P (2015) The case of the missing laureate: The communication geography of the 2010 Nobel Peace Prize. In S Mains, J Cupples and C Lukinbeal (eds) *Mediated Geographies and Geographies of Media.* Dordrecht: Springer, pp. 313–327.

Almanza R and Cruz J D (2013) La vida en El Carmen. *La Prensa* 18 August http://www.laprensa.com.ni/2013/08/18/seccion-domingo/158973-la-vida-en-el-carmen (Accessed 2 November 2015).

Althusser, L (1969). *For Marx*. Harmondsworth, UK: Penguin.

Alvarez C F (2015) Pistolero de Metrocentro: Mónica Zalaquett me contactó para echarle leña al fuego. *El 19 Digital* 5 September http://www.el19digital.com/articulos/ver/titulo:33241-pistolero-de-metrocentro-monica-zalaquett-me-contacto-para-echarle-lena-al-fuego (Accessed 1 December 2015).

Alvarez L (2016) Conflictos indígenas ignorados por diputados orteguistas. *La Prensa* 20 March http://www.laprensa.com.ni/2016/03/20/politica/2005705-conflictos-indigenas-son-ignorados-por-los-diputados-orteguistas (Accessed 8 June 2016).

Alvarez R (2016a) Metas ambientales del Marena no dan esperanza. *La Prensa* 8 January http://www.laprensa.com.ni/2016/01/08/nacionales/1965645-metas-ambientales-del-marena-no-dan-esperanza (Accessed 27 January 2016).

Alvarez R (2016b) Gobierno presiona a ramas por Canal. *La Prensa* 11 January http://www.laprensa.com.ni/2016/01/11/nacionales/1967324-gobierno-presiona-a-ramas-por-canal (Accessed 2 February 2016).

Alvarez Hidalgo W (2016) Poder de compra aún es menor que en 2006. *La Prensa* 18 January.

Álvarez L and Chamorro E (2016) Corte Suprema de Justicia quita el PLI a Eduardo Montealegre. *La Prensa* 8 June http://www.laprensa.com.ni/2016/06/08/politica/2048525-sala-constitucional-de-la-csj-por-resolver-litis-de-representacion-del-pli (Accessed 7 August 2016).

A Mano Limpia (2015) Escándalo de pedofilia envuelve al presidente de Nicaragua, Daniel Ortega [video] *América Tevé*, 8 October http://www.americateve.com/escandalo-pedofilia-envuelve-al-presidente-nicaragua-daniel-ortega-n881996 (Accessed 3 March 2016).

Antonio M (2008) ¿De quiénes y para quiénes son las tierras costeñas? *Envío* 321 http://www.envio.org.ni/articulo/3904 (Accessed 8 November 2015).

AP (2016a) Nicaragua expels six environmental activists accused of handling explosives. *The Guardian* 28 June https://www.theguardian.com/world/2016/jun/28/nicaragua-expels-environmental-activists-explosives (Accessed 7 August 2016).

J. Cupples and K. Glynn, *Shifting Nicaraguan Mediascapes*,
SpringerBriefs in Latin American Studies,
https://doi.org/10.1007/978-3-319-64319-9

AP (2016b) Nicaraguan president's wife tapped to be his running mate. *Fox News* 2 August http://www.nytimes.com/aponline/2016/08/02/world/americas/ap-lt-nicaragua-presidential-election.html?_r=0 (Accessed 7 August 2016).

Bangkukuk Taik (2015) Bangkukuk Taik an indigenous Rama community and the Nicaraguan interoceanic grand canal [YouTube] https://www.youtube.com/watch?v=IIM-D–2lb4 (Accessed 25 November 2015).

Bangkukuk Taik (2016) We Do Not Consent! - The indigenous struggle against the Grand Canal of Nicaragua [Vimeo] https://vimeo.com/174291184 (Accessed 6 December 2016).

Bárcenas F (2015) Reforma agraria en la Costa Caribe. *Confidencial* 7 October http://confidencial.com.ni/reforma-agraria-en-la-costa-caribe/ (Accessed 10 October 2015).

Belli G (2015) Por sus hechos los conoceréis. *Confidencial* 7 September http://confidencial.com.ni/por-sus-hechos-los-conocereis/ (Accessed 1 December 2015).

Belli Pereira H (2013) Una bofetada para todos. *La Prensa* 8 July http://www.laprensa.com.ni/2013/07/08/opinion/153837-una-bofetada-para-todos (Accessed 19 November).

Brysk A (2000) *From Tribal Village to Global Village: Indian Rights and International Relations in Latin America.* Palo Alto: Stanford University Press.

Burgess J and Green J (2009) *YouTube: Online Video and Participatory Culture.* Cambridge: Polity.

Carballo W, Chavarría Molina R A, Cristancho Cuesta A, Jover Segura A, Meza Meetabel D, Oliva K, Orozco Andrade P A (2014) *Entre la censura y la discriminación : Centroamérica amenazada: Diagnóstico sobre violaciones a los derechos humanos de periodistas y medios comunitarios de la región.* San Salvador: Fundación Comunicándonos.

Carroll R (2008) Intellectuals condemn authoritarian Ortega. *The Guardian* 24 June http://www.theguardian.com/world/2008/jun/24/2 (Accessed 4 March 2016).

Castells M (2007) Communication, power and counter-power in the network society. *International Journal of Communication* 1: 238–266.

Castells M (2012) *Networks of Outrage and Hope: Social Movements in the Internet Age.* Cambridge: Polity.

Cavenaze N (2015) "Illiberal": The white backlash word. *Racism Review* November 15 http://www.racismreview.com/blog/2015/11/15/illiberal-the-white-backlash-word/ (Accessed 21 November).

CEJIL (2015) Comisión Interamericana de Derechos Humanos exige a Nicaragua la protección de los miskitos de la Costa Caribe Norte [press release] 17 October https://cejil.org/comunicados/comision-interamericana-de-derechos-humanos-exige-a-nicaragua-la-proteccion-de-los-miski (Accessed 29 November 2015).

Cejudhcan derechos humanos (2015a) Documental CEJUDHCAN [YouTube] 17 February https://www.youtube.com/watch?v=uSiByOazZ9Y (Accessed 22 November 2015).

Cejudhcan derechos humanos (2015b) Deadly conditions on the Miskito Coast [YouTube] 6 July https://www.youtube.com/watch?v=jDMdPHQ-Jd0 (Accessed 25 November).

Cejudhcan derechos humanos (2015c) Situación del territorio indígena Wangki Twi Tasba Raya [YouTube] 15 July https://www.youtube.com/watch?v=lG4D9HF1KXo (Accessed 26 November 2015).

Cejudhcan derechos humanos (2015d) Adolescentes indígenas piden ayuda a través de su canto ante la invasión de colonos [YouTube] 7 September https://www.youtube.com/watch?v=fbi6Qk8rUI0 (Accessed 26 November 2015).

Cenidh Nicaragua (2015) Juan Herbacio, Presentador la Revista La Voz de la Verdad, Radio Yapti -Tasba, Bilwi [YouTube] 12 November https://www.youtube.com/watch?v=uFvNNk_e3RI (Accessed 15 November 2015).

CENIDH (2016) Organizaciones de las Américas preocupadas por destitución de diputados. *CENIDH* 4 August http://www.cenidh.org/noticias/916/ (Accessed 7 August 2016).

Centro Humboldt (2014) *Valoraciones Socio-Ambientales de la Ruta Seleccionada para la Construcción del Gran Canal Interoceánico por Nicaragua.* Centro Humboldt: Managua http://www.slideshare.net/centroalexandervonhumboldt/resumen-ejecutivo-estudio-41540677 (Accessed 4 March 2016).

Cerda A and Miranda W (2016) El mazazo de la abstención. *Confidencial* 12 November http://confidencial.com.ni/mazazo-la-abstencion/ (Accessed 12 December 2016).

Chamorro E (2015a) "El Gobierno quiere terminar con nosotros". *La Prensa* 16 September http://www.laprensa.com.ni/2015/09/16/nacionales/1902632-el-gobierno-quiere-terminar-con-nosotros (Accessed 28 November 2015).

Chamorro E (2015b) Ejército habría emboscado a indígenas en Waspam. *La Prensa* 16 September http://www.laprensa.com.ni/2015/09/16/nacionales/1902585-ejercito-embosca-a-indigenas (Accessed 28 November 2015).

Chamorro E and Castillo J (2015) Orteguistas cierran con discurso del "Chocolatito". *La Prensa* 28 October http://www.laprensa.com.ni/2015/10/28/nacionales/1926701-orteguistas-cierran-con-discurso-del-chocolatito (Accessed 1 December 2015).

Chamorro Mendieta E (2016) Pedro Reyes renunciará a candidatura presidencial. *La Prensa* 9 September http://www.laprensa.com.ni/2016/09/19/politica/2102620-pedro-reyes-renunciara-candidatura-presidencial (Accessed 13 December 2016).

Chávez K (2015) Chocolatito invita a tod@s a participar en la Caminata Trabajo y Paz… Unida, Nicaragua Triunfa! *El 19 Digital* 26 October http://www.el19digital.com/articulos/ver/titulo:35009-chocolatito-invita-a-tods-a-participar-en-la-caminata-trabajo-y-paz-unida-nicaragua-triunfa (Accessed 1 December 2015).

Chedekel L (2015) Kidney disease epidemic among Nicaragua sugarcane workers: School of Public Health study finds occupational link. *BU Today* 10 March. http://www.bu.edu/today/2015/kidney-disease-epidemic-among-sugarcane-workers/ (Accessed 19 June 2016).

Comunidad Negra Creole Indígena de Bluefields (2012) *Diagnóstico del Territorio de la Comunidad Negra Creole Indígena de Bluefields.* Available at http://www.calpi-nicaragua.org/diagnostico-del-territorio-de-la-comunidad-negra-creole-indigena-de-bluefields/ (Accessed 31 May 2016).

Confidencial (2015) Armado dispara contra manifestantes en miércoles de protesta [YouTube] 2 September https://www.youtube.com/watch?v=cQl6awttglo&feature=youtu.be (Accessed 1 December 2015).

Confidencial (2016) Denuncian de ilegal el acuerdo de arrendamiento para la construcción del canal interoceánico [YouTube] 20 May https://www.youtube.com/watch?v=uaR07qkKzGw (Accessed 9 June 2016).

Confidencial (2017) HKND reduce al mínimo su presencia en Nicaragua. 30 March https://confidencial.com.ni/hknd-reduce-al-minimo-presencia-nicaragua/ (Accessed 1 April 2017).

Contreras D (2016) Ortega está desmantelando la democracia como un dinasta: Víctor Hugo Tinoco. *Milenio* 4 August http://www.milenio.com/internacional/Ortega-desmantelando-democracia-dinasta_0_786521358.html (Accessed 7 August 2016).

Cordero M (2016) Las 50 mujeres más poderosas de Centroamérica. *Forbes* 26 July http://www.forbes.com.mx/las-50-mujeres-mas-poderosas-centroamerica-3/#gs.4Qb34Wk (Accessed 7 August 2016).

Cruz J D (2016) Áreas protegidas siguen en riesgo. *El Nuevo Diario* 21 January http://www.elnuevodiario.com.ni/nacionales/382809-areas-protegidas-siguen-riesgo/ (Accessed 23 January 2016).

Cunningham Kain M (2006) *Racism and Ethnic Discrimination in Nicaragua.* Bilwi: Centro para la Autonomía y Desarrollo de los Pueblos Indígenas.

Cupples J (2002) *Disrupting Discourses and (Re)formulating Identities: The Politics of Single Motherhood in Postrevolutionary Nicaragua.* Unpublished PhD thesis, University of Canterbury.

Cupples J (2009) Rethinking electoral geography: Spaces and practices of democracy in Nicaragua. *Transactions of the Institute of British Geographers* 34(1): 110–124.

Cupples J (2013) *Latin American Development.* London: Routledge.
Cupples J and Glynn K (2013) Postdevelopment television? Cultural citizenship and the mediation of Africa in contemporary TV drama. *Annals of the Association of American Geographers* 103 (4): 1003–1021.
Cupples J (2014) Nicaragua: Travels in hyperreality [blog] 1 February https://juliecupples.wordpress.com/2014/02/01/nicaragua-travels-in-hyperreality/ (Accessed 20 August 2016).
Cupples J and Glynn K (2014a) Indigenizing and decolonizing higher education on Nicaragua's Atlantic Coast. *Singapore Journal of Tropical Geography* 35: 56–71.
Cupples J and Glynn K (2014b) The mediation and remediation of disaster: Hurricanes Katrina and Felix in/and the new media environment. *Antipode* 46(2): 359–381.
Cupples J and Glynn K (2016) Neoliberalism, surveillance and media convergence. In S Springer, K Birch and J MacLeavy (eds) *The Routledge Handbook of Neoliberalism.* London: Routledge, pp. 161–175.
Cupples J, Glynn K and Lee D (forthcoming) La negociación de identidades negras en los medios de comunicación convergentes en la Costa Caribe de Nicaragua. In R Cáceres and P Lovejoy (eds.), *El significado de la negritud.* San José: Editorial Universidad de Costa Rica.
Cupples J and Larios I (2005) Gender, elections, terrorism: the geopolitical enframing of the 2001 Nicaraguan elections. *Political Geography* 24: 317–339.
Das V (2004) The signature of the state: The paradox of illegibility. In V Das and D Poole (eds) *Anthropology in the Margins of the State*. Santa Fe: School of American Research Press, pp. 225–254.
Dayan D (2009) Sharing and showing: Television as monstration. *The ANNALS of the American Academy of Political and Social Science* 625(Sept.): 19–31.
Dennis P A (2004) *The Miskitu people of Awastara.* Austin: University of Texas Press.
Dussel E (1977) *Filosofia de Liberación.* México: Edicol.
de Sousa Santos B (2004) The World Social Forum: Toward a counter-hegemonic globalisation (Part I). In J Sen, A Anand, A Escobar and P Waterman (eds) *World Social Forum: Challenging Empires.* New Delhi: Viveka Foundation, pp. 235–245.
de Sousa Santos B (2014) *Epistemologies of the South.* Boulder: Paradigm Publishers.
Duncan Q (2012) *El Pueblo Afrodescendiente: Diálogos con el Abuelo Juan Bautista Yayah.* Bloomington: Palibrio.
El 19 Digital (2015) Empresa B2Gold destaca restablecimiento del orden institucional en Mina El Limón. *El 19 Digital* 17 October https://www.el19digital.com/articulos/ver/titulo:34701-empresa-b2gold-destaca-restablecimiento-del-orden-institucional-en-mina-el-limon (Accessed 1 December 2015).
El Nuevo Diario (2013) Xochilt Ocampo despojada de su escaño. *El Nuevo Diario* 24 June http://www.elnuevodiario.com.ni/politica/289801-xochilt-ocampo-despojada-su-escano/ (Accessed 19 November 2015).
ERM (2015) *Environmental and Social Impact Assessement: Canal de Nicaragua.* Available at http://hknd-group.com/portal.php?mod=view&aid=293 (Accessed 27 January 2016).
Escobar A (2007) Worlds and knowledges otherwise. *Cultural Studies* 21(2–3): 179–210.
Escobar A (2010) Latin America at a crossroads. *Cultural Studies* 24(1): 1–65.
Ettlinger N and Hartman C D (2015) Post/neo/liberalism in relational perspective. *Political Geography* 48: 37–48.
Feinberg R (2011) Daniel Ortega and Nicaragua's Soft Authoritarianism. *Foreign Affairs* 2 November https://www.foreignaffairs.com/articles/nicaragua/2011-11-02/daniel-ortega-and-nicaraguas-soft-authoritarianism (Accessed 4 March 2016).
Fendt L (2016) Indigenous and Afro-Caribbeans claim they were forced to negotiate over Nicaragua Canal. *Tico Times* 14 January http://www.ticotimes.net/2016/01/14/indigenous-afro-caribbeans-claim-forced-negotiate-nicaragua-canal (Accessed 3 February 2015).
Field L W. (1999) *The Grimace of Macho Ratón: Artisans, Identity, and Nation in Late-Twentieth Century Western Nicaragua*. Durham: Duke University Press.

Fiske J (1998). Surveilling the city: Whiteness, the Black man and democratic totalitarianism. *Theory Culture & Society* 15(2): 67–88.
Fiske J (2016a). *Power Plays, Power Works*, Second Ed. London: Routledge.
Fiske J (2016b). *Media Matters: Race and Gender in U.S. Politics*, Second Ed. London: Routledge.
Flores J (2015) "Mi niña fue violada por Daniel Ortega". *Diario Las Américas* 22 October http://www.diariolasamericas.com/5051_portada-america-latina/3410807_nina-fue-violada-daniel-ortega.html (Accessed 3 March 2016).
Frank Gómez E (2014) Prólogo. In DMairena (ed) *Demarcación y Titulación de Territorios Indígenas: La Reivindicación deDerechos Ancestrales*. Bilwi:Centro para la Autonomía y Desarrollo de los Pueblos Indígenas.
Front Line Defenders (2015) Nicaragua: Ataques contra defensores de derechos humanos que trabajan con la comunidad Wangki Twi. *Front Line Defenders* 22 September https://www.frontlinedefenders.org/es/node/29683 (Accessed 29 November 2015).
Finley-Brook M (2011) "We are the owners": Autonomy and natural resources in Northeastern Nicaragua. In L Baracco (ed) *National Integration and Contested Autonomy: The Caribbean Coast of Nicaragua.* New York: Algora, pp. 302–332.
Finley-Brook M and Offen K (2009) Bounding the commons: Land demarcation in northeastern Nicaragua. *Bulletin of Latin American Research* 28(3): 343–363.
Flores J (2015) Miskitos denuncian al régimen sandinista en Estados Unidos. *La Prensa* 19 September http://www.laprensa.com.ni/2015/09/19/nacionales/1904657-miskitos-denuncian-al-regimen-sandinista-en-estados-unidos (Accessed 29 November 2015).
Funez S (2015) Conflicto entre miskitos y colonos [YouTube] 7 September https://www.youtube.com/watch?v=5js3h2bINO4 (Accessed 23 November).
Galo Romero H (2016) Nicaragua, sin actualizar el estado de sus bosques. *El Nuevo Diario* 4 January http://www.elnuevodiario.com.ni/nacionales/381185-nicaragua-actualizar-estado-sus-bosques/ (Accessed 27 January 2015).
García Peralta M (2015) El "quita y pon" de alcaldes. *La Prensa* 8 November http://www.laprensa.com.ni/2015/11/08/politica/1932823-16473 (Accessed 10 November 2015).
Gehl R (2009) YouTube as archive: Who will curate this digital Wunderkammer? *International Journal of Cultural Studies* 12(1): 43–60.
Ginsburg F (1991) Indigenous media: Faustian contract or global village? *Cultural Anthropology* 6 (1): 92–112.
Glynn K (2000) *Tabloid Culture: Trash Taste, Popular Power, and the Transformation of American Television*. Durham: Duke University Press.
Glynn K and Cupples J (2011) Indigenous mediaspace and the production of (trans)locality on Nicaragua's Mosquito Coast. *Television and New Media* 12(2): 101–135.
Glynn K and Tyson A F (2007) Indigeneity, media and cultural globalization: The case of Mataku, or the Maori X-Files. *International Journal of Cultural Studies* 10(2): 205–224.
Goett J (2006) *Diasporic Identities, Autochthonous Rights: Race, Gender, and the Cultural Politics of Creole Land Rights in Nicaragua.* Unpublished PhD dissertation, University of Texas-Austin.
Goldsmith A J (2010) Policing's new visibility. *British Journal of Criminology* 50: 914–934.
González A (2016) Francisca Ramírez: "A mí no me han quitado los huevos" *La Prensa* 3 July http://www.laprensa.com.ni/2016/07/03/suplemento/la-prensa-domingo/2061597-entrevista-con-francisca-ramirez (Accessed 7 August 2016).
González J (2015) Mina El Limón vuelve a la normalidad. *El Nuevo Diario* 20 October http://www.elnuevodiario.com.ni/nacionales/374177-mina-limon-vuelve-normalidad/ (Accessed 3 March 2016).
González N (2016a) Solo quedará el "esqueleto" de la oficina del PNUD en Nicaragua. *La Prensa* 9 February http://www.laprensa.com.ni/2016/02/09/nacionales/1983251-solo-quedara-esqueleto-la-oficina-del-pnud-nicaragua (Accessed 9 June 2016).

González N (2016b) Nicaragua pierde US$60 millones en ayuda. *La Prensa* 10 February http://www.laprensa.com.ni/2016/02/10/nacionales/1983805-nicaragua-pierde-us60-millones-en-ayuda (Accessed 9 June 2016).

Gordon E T, Gurdián G C, and Hale C R (2003) Rights, resources, and the social memory of struggle: Reflections on a study of indigenous and black community land rights on Nicaragua's Atlantic Coast. *Human Organization* 62(4): 369–381.

Gould J (1998) *To Die in This Way: Nicaraguan Indians and the Myth of Mestizaje 1880-1965.* Durham: Duke University Press.

Grigsby, W. 2005. Elecciones en la Costa Caribe (1): Entre el abandono, la droga y la apatía. *Envío* 285. http://www.envio.org.ni/articulo/3142 (accessed November 15, 2008).

Grosfoguel R (2012) Decolonizing Western Uni-versalisms: Decolonial Pluri-versalism from Aimé Césaire to the Zapatistas. *Transmodernity: Journal of Peripheral Cultural Production of the Luso-Hispanic World* 1(3): 88–104.

Grosfoguel R (2015) Epistemic racism/sexism, westernized universities and the four genocides/epistemicides of the long sixteenth century. In S Rodríguez Maeso and M Araújo (eds) *Eurocentrism, Racism and Knowledge.* Basingstoke: Palgrave Macmillan, pp. 23–46.

Gross M and McGoey L (2015) Introduction. In M Gross and L McGoey (eds) *The Routledge International Handbook of Ignorance Studies.* Abingdon: Routledge, pp. 1–14.

Grossman C (2001) Awas Tingni v. Nicaragua: A landmark case for the Inter-American system. *Human Rights Brief* 8 (3): 2–4, 8.

Gurdián G and Kauffmann M (2002) Nicaribe soy: El Caribe nicaragüense en las lentes de Claudia Gordillo y María José Alvarez. *WANI: Revista del Caribe Nicaragüense* (30): 32–41.

Hale C (1992) *Resistance and Contradiction: Miskitu Indians and the Nicaraguan State, 1894–1987.* Stanford: Stanford University Press.

Hale C (2005) Neoliberal multiculturalism: The remaking of cultural rights and racial dominance in Central America. *PoLAR* 28(1): 10–29.

Hall S (1981) The whites of their eyes: Racist ideologies and the media. In G Bridges and R Brunt (eds) *Silver Linings: Some Strategies for the Eighties.* London: Lawrence and Wishart, pp. 28–52.

Hall S (1996 [1986]) Gramsci's relevance for the study of race and ethnicity. In D Morley and KH Chen (eds) *Stuart Hall: Critical Dialogues in Cultural Studies.* London: Routledge, pp. 411–441.

Hall S (2006 [1981]) Notes on deconstructing the popular. In J Storey (ed) *Cultural Theory and Popular Culture: A Reader,* 3rd ed. Harlow: Pearson, pp. 477–487.

Hall S, Critcher C, Jefferson T, Clarke J and Roberts B (2013) *Policing the Crisis: Mugging, the State and Law and Order*, Second Edition. Houndmills, UK: Palgrave Macmillan.

Helms M (1971) *Asang: Adaptations to culture contact in a Miskitu community.* Gainesville: University of Florida Press.

Himpele J (2008) *Circuits of Culture: Media, Politics, and Indigenous Identity in the Andes.* Minneapolis: University of Minnesota Press.

Hooker J (2005a) Indigenous inclusion/black exclusion: Race, ethnicity and multicultural citizenship in Latin America. *Journal of Latin American Studies* 37(2): 285–310.

Hooker J (2005b) "Beloved enemies": Race and official mestizo nationalism in Nicaragua. *Latin American Research Review* 40(3): 14–39.

Huete-Pérez J A, Meyer A and Alvarez P J (2015) Rethink the Nicaragua canal. *Science* 347 (6220): 355.

INIDE (2015) Resultados de la "Encuesta Nacional de Hogares sobre Medición de Nivel de Vida 2014". Managua: Instituto Nacional de Información de Desarrollo.

Jenkins H (2006) *Convergence culture: Where Old and New Media Collide.* New York: NYU Press.

Jenkins H (2016) Youth voice, media, and political engagement: Introducing the core concepts. In H Jenkins, S Shresthova, L Gamber-Thompson, N Kligler-Vilenchik, and A Zimmerman (eds) *By Any Media Necessary: The New Youth Activism.* NYU Press. Kindle Edition.

Jenkins H, Ford S and Green J (2013) *Spreadable Media: Creating Value and Meaning in a Networked Culture*. New York: NYU Press.

Joel EMC (2016) Situación actual del periodismo en la Costa Caribe de Nicaragua. [YouTube] 29 February (originally broadcast on TV7, Bilwi in August 2015) https://www.youtube.com/watch?v=8GHvCtubHGQ (Accessed 8 June 2016).

Jones S (2016) Nicaraguan president accused of nepotism over wife's VP ticket. *The Guardian* 3 August https://www.theguardian.com/world/2016/aug/03/daniel-ortega-nicaraguan-sandinista-president-rosario-murillo (Accessed 7 August 2016).

Jubb N (2014) Love, family values and reconciliation for all, but what about rights, justice and citizenship for women? The FSLN, the women's movement, and violence against women inNicaragua. *Bulletin of Latin American Research* 33(3): 289–304.

Juris J (2008) *Networking Futures: The Movements Against Corporate Globalization*. Durham, NC: Duke University Press.

Kampwirth K (2008) Abortion, antifeminism, and the return of Daniel Ortega: In Nicaragua, leftist politics? *Latin American Perspectives* 35(6): 122–136.

Kilpatrick K (2016) Indigenous and Afro-Caribbeans say Nicaragua coercing them on canal. *Al Jazeera America* 12 January http://america.aljazeera.com/articles/2016/1/12/indigenous-leaders-say-nicaragua-pressuring-them-to-agree-to-canal.html (Accessed 3 February 2016).

Kipnis L (1992) (Male) desire and (female) disgust: Reading *Hustler*. In L Grossberg, C Nelson and P Treichler (eds) *Cultural Studies*. New York: Routledge, pp. 373–391.

Lacayo Ortiz I (2016) FSLN ordena cierre del noticiero en Bluefields. *La Prensa* 10 October http://www.laprensa.com.ni/2016/10/10/politica/2114751-diputado-orteguista-cierra-noticiero-de-periodista-en-bluefields (Accessed 12 December 2016).

La Jornada (2015) Nicaragua: megaproyecto peligroso. *La Jornada* 29 October 2015 http://www.jornada.unam.mx/2015/10/29/edito (Accessed 18 November 2015).

Lakhani N (2015) Lies and statistics. *Index on Censorship* 44(1): 80–83.

Lakhani N (2016) Nicaragua suppresses opposition to ensure one-party election, critics say. *The Guardian* 26 June https://www.theguardian.com/world/2016/jun/26/nicaragua-opposition-daniel-ortega-presidential-election (Accessed 7 August 2016).

La Prensa (2015a) Denuncia de periodistas ante el CENIDH [YouTube] 11 November https://www.youtube.com/watch?v=YwPKGIgqXE8 (Accessed 15 November 2015).

La Prensa (2015b) Periodistas independientes en Bilwi son amenazados. *La Prensa TV* 12 November http://www.laprensa.com.ni/2015/11/12/lptv/1935745-periodistas-independientes-en-bilwi-son-amenazados (Accessed 13 November 2015).

La Prensa (2015c) Cuatro años de prisión a Samir Maramoros. *La Prensa* 11 September http://www.laprensa.com.ni/2015/09/11/nacionales/1900161-cuatro-anos-de-prision-a-samir-maramoros (Accessed 10 March 2016).

La Voz del Sandinismo (2015) Denuncian acciones contra derecho a propiedad comunal http://www.lavozdelsandinismo.com/nicaragua/2015-09-21/denuncian-acciones-contra-derecho-a-propiedad-comunal-texto/ (Accessed 29 November 2015).

Lenzerini F (2014) *The Culturalization of Human Rights Law*. Oxford: Oxford University Press.

León C S (2014) Denuncian racismo en promoción comercial. *La Prensa* 22 January http://www.laprensa.com.ni/2014/01/22/departamentales/179310 (Accessed 22 January 2014).

Leyden-Sussler L (2014) Nicaragua: On the brink of dictatorship. *World Policy Blog* 26 February http://www.worldpolicy.org/blog/2014/02/25/nicaragua-brink-dictatorship (Accessed 4 March 2016).

López E (2015) "Arde" Mina El Limón. *La Prensa* 8 May http://www.laprensa.com.ni/2015/05/08/departamentales/1828397-arde-mina-el-limon (Accessed 1 December 2015).

López I (2016) CSE amenaza a usuarios de las redes sociales en Nicaragua. *La Prensa* 8 August http://www.laprensa.com.ni/2016/08/08/politica/2080144-cse-amenaza-a-usuarios-de-las-redes-sociales (Accessed 12 December 2016).

Madrid R L, Hunter W and Weyland K (2010) The policies and performance of the contestatory and moderate left. In K Weyland, R L Madrid and W Hunter (eds) *Leftist Governments in Latin America: Successes and Shortcomings*. Cambridge: Cambridge University Press, pp. 140–180.

Mairena D (2014) *Demarcación y Titulación de Territorios Indigenas: La Reivindicación de Derechos Ancestrales*. Bilwi: Centro para la Autonomía y Desarrollo de los Pueblos Indígenas.

Manzano V (2014) *The Age of Youth in Argentina: Culture, Politics, and Sexuality from Perón to Videla*. Chapel Hill: The University of North Carolina Press.

Marlon Moreno (2015) De esta es la paz y la felicidad que habla el animal que tenemos de presidente [Facebook video] 28 May https://www.facebook.com/100008517287841/videos/1454446628182566/ (Accessed 1 December 2015).

Martín-Barbero J (2011) From Latin America: Diversity, globalization and convergence. *Westminster Papers in Communication and Culture* 8(1): 39–64.

MASTA (2015) Nota de solidaridad [Press release] 24 September Puerto Lempira: Miskitu Asla Takankahttp://www.mastamiskitu.org/index.php/noticias/94-solidaridad-con-ta-upla-brooklynrivera(Accessed 25 September 2015).

McConnell S A (2014) The 2011 presidential and legislative elections in Nicaragua. *Electoral Studies* 34: 300–303.

McGoey L (2007) On the will to ignorance in bureaucracy. *Economy and Society* 36(2): 212–235.

McGregor J and TeAwa J (1996) Racism and the news media. In P Spoonley, D Pearson and C Macpherson (eds) *Nga Patai: Racism and Ethnic Relations in Aotearoa/New Zealand*. Palmerston North: Dunmore Press, pp. 235–246.

Membreño C (2016) Science: el Canal divide a Nicaragua. *Confidencial* 21 January http://confidencial.com.ni/science-el-canal-divide-a-nicaragua/ (Accessed 24 January 2016).

Mignolo W (2005) *The Idea of Latin America*. Malden: Blackwell.

Mills C (1997) *The Racial Contract*. Ithaca: Cornell University Press.

Mills C (2015) Global white ignorance. In M Gross and L McGoey (eds) *The Routledge International Handbook of Ignorance Studies*. Abingdon: Routledge, pp. 217–227.

Miranda Aburto W (2015) Confesiones prefabricadas. *Confidencial* 7 September http://confidencial.com.ni/confesiones-prefabricadas/ (Accessed 16 September 2015).

Miranda Aburto W (2016) Gobierno de Ortega expulsa a director de Freedom House. *Confidencial* 3 February http://confidencial.com.ni/expulsan-del-pais-a-director-de-freedom-house/ (Accessed 3 February 2016).

Mirzoeff N (2005) *Watching Babylon: The War in Iraq and Global Visual Culture*. New York: Routledge.

Mollett S (2013) Mapping deception: The politics of mapping Miskito and Garifuna space in Honduras. *Annals of the Association of American Geographers* 103(5): 1227–1241.

Moncada R and Silva J A (2015) US$3.3 millones en los "árboles de la vida", *La Prensa* 3 November http://www.laprensa.com.ni/2015/11/03/nacionales/1929807-us3-3-millones-en-los-arboles-de-la-vida (Accessed 5 November 2015).

Montenegro Baena L (2015a) Frente al canal: De la descolonización de la autonomía a la independencia del Caribe nicaragüense [blog] 13 August http://montenegrobaena.blogspot.co.uk/2015/08/frente-al-canal-de-la-descolonizacion.html (Accessed 8 June 2016).

Montenegro Baena L (2015b) Legislar desde el espiritú de la autonomía: Desde abajo [blog] 29 October http://montenegrobaena.blogspot.co.uk/2015/10/legislar-desde-el-espiritu-de-la.html (Accessed 8 June 2016).

Mosquera J (2016) Nicaragua: del tirano de Somoza al sátrapa de Ortega. *Las 2 Orillas* 1 August http://www.las2orillas.co/nicaragua-del-tirano-somoza-al-satrapa-ortega/ (Accessed 7 August 2016).

Navarrete J (2015) La batalla del periodismo independiente. *Confidencial* 8 September http://confidencial.com.ni/la-batalla-del-periodismo-independiente/ (Accessed 27 October 2015).

Navas L (2015) Ortega escondió invasión de tierras. *La Prensa* 28 September http://www.laprensa.com.ni/2015/09/28/nacionales/1909618-ortega-escondio-invasion-de-tierras (Accessed 28 September 2015).

Navas L and Álvarez L (2015) Siete años del fraude en municipales de 2008. *La Prensa* 11 November http://www.laprensa.com.ni/2015/11/10/politica/1934047-siete-anos-del-fraude-en-municipales-de-2008-2 (Accessed 11 November 2015).
Navarro A (2015) Hambre y abandono en comunidades RAAN. *Confidencial* 16 October http://confidencial.com.ni/hambre-y-abandono-en-comunidades-raan/ (Accessed 16 October 2015).
Nicaragua Hoy (2015) Zalaquett recibe gran apoyo en redes sociales ante trama oficialista. *Nicaragua Hoy* 6 September http://www.nicaraguahoy.info/zalaquett-recibe-gran-apoyo-en-redes-sociales-ante-trama-oficialista/ (Accessed 22 September 2015).
Nietschmann B (1989) *The Unknown War: The Miskito Nation, Nicaragua, and the United States*. Lanham, MD: University Press of America.
Nietschmann B (1995) Defending the Miskito reefs with maps and GPS. *Cultural Survival Quarterly* 18(4): 34–37.
Nole Importa (2012) Daniel Ortega *es "el hazme reír"* [YouTube] https://www.youtube.com/watch?v=hLSNdJtnoOA (Accessed 3 March 2016).
Olivares I (2015a) Gobierno impone un "apagón informativo". *Confidencial* 6 October http://confidencial.com.ni/gobierno-oculta-datos-de-pobreza/ (Accessed 4 November 2015).
Olivares I (2015b) Encuesta oficial: pobreza bajó de 42.5% a 29.6%. *Confidencial* 6 October http://confidencial.com.ni/pobreza-bajo-de-42-5-a-29-6/ (Accessed 14 November 2015).
Onda Local (2016a) Carlos Wilson Billis [YouTube] 6 May https://www.youtube.com/watch?v=ny-mbVj_9ZU (Accessed 9 June 2016).
Onda Local (2016b) Monkey Point Allen Clair [YouTube] 17 May https://www.youtube.com/watch?v=R2Y6VzRN8eQ (Accessed 9 June 2016).
Onda Local (2016c) Bankukuk Taik Comunitarios [YouTube] 17 May https://www.youtube.com/watch?v=1o4uSBFj34I (Accessed 9 June 2016).
Orozco P and López J (2014) Nicaragua: La relativa calma. In Carballo W, Chavarría Molina R A, Cristancho Cuesta A, Jover Segura A, Meza Meetabel D, Oliva K, Patricia Amanda Orozco Andrade P A (eds) *Entre la censura y la discrimación : Centroamérica amenazada: Diagnóstico sobre violaciones a los derechos humanos de periodistas y medios comunitarios de la region*. San Salvador: Fundación Comunicándonos, pp 127–180.
Orozco P (2015) Los medios locales están invisibilizados y amenazados. Envío 399 http://www.envio.org.ni/articulo/5017 (Accessed 20 November 2017).
Ortega Ramírez P (2014) La autonomía es la revolución en la Costa Caribe. *El 19 Digital* 1 November http://www.el19digital.com/articulos/ver/titulo:23577-la-autonomia-es-la-revolucion-en-la-costa-caribe (Accessed 4 September 2015).
Peet R (2009) *Unholy Trinity: The IMF, World Bank and WTO.* 2nd ed. London: Zed Books.
Pineda B (2006) *Shipwrecked Identities: Navigating Race on Nicaragua's Mosquito Coast.* New Brunswick: Rutgers University Press.
Prado Reyes Y (2016) Firman acuerdo de consentimiento para uso de tierras del Gobierno Territorial Rama y Kriol. *19 Digital* 3 May http://www.el19digital.com/articulos/ver/titulo:41492-firman-acuerdo-de-consentimiento-para-uso-de-tierras-del-gobierno-territorial-rama-y-kriol (Accessed 9 June 2016).
Proctor R N and Schiebinger L (2008) Preface. In R N Proctor and L Schiebinger (eds) *Agnotology: The Making and Unmaking of Ignorance.* Stanford: Stanford University Press, pp.vii-viii.
Pulido L (2016) Flint, environmental racism, and racial capitalism. *Capitalism Nature Socialism* 27(3): 1–16.
Quijano A (2007) Coloniality and modernity/rationality. *Cultural Studies* 21(2–3): 168–178.
Ramírez S (2007) *Tambor Olvidado.* San José: Aguilar.
Redacción Central (2015) Denuncian ola de destituciones en RAAN. *Trinchera de la Noticia* 19 May http://www.trincheraonline.com/2015/05/19/denuncian-ola-de-destituciones-en-raan/ (Accessed 4 September 2015).

Reuters (2016) Been watching House of Cards? Nicaraguan President Ortega picks his WIFE as his running mate. *The Daily Mail* 3 August http://www.dailymail.co.uk/news/article-3721011/Nicaraguas-Ortega-picks-wife-running-mate-pledges-joint-rule.html (Accessed 7 August 2016).

Rezaye Álvarez M (2016) Ramas y Kriol denuncian acuerdo ilegal con el Gobierno. *La Prensa* 3 May http://www.laprensa.com.ni/2016/05/03/nacionales/2028754-ramas-kriol-denuncian-acuerdo-ilegal-gobierno (Accessed 9 June 2016).

Rincón O (2014) Buenos periodistas, malos medios. *Nueva Sociedad* 249: 97–100.

Rivera Cusicanqui S (2012) Ch'ixinakax utxiwa: A reflection on practices and discourses of decolonization. *South Atlantic Quarterly* 111(1): 95–109.

Rockwell R and Janus N (2003) *Media power in Central America.* Urbana, IL: University of Illinois Press.

Rodríguez Maeso S and Marta Araújo M (2015) Eurocentrism, political struggles and the entrenched *will-to-ignorance.* In S Rodríguez Maeso and M Araújo (eds) *Eurocentrism, Racism and Knowledge.* Basingstoke: Palgrave Macmillan, pp. 1–22.

Romero E (2015a) Aumentan riesgos para el periodismo. *La Prensa* 13 November http://www.laprensa.com.ni/2015/11/13/nacionales/1935930-aumentan-riesgos-para-el-periodismo (Accessed 23 November 2015).

Romero E (2015b) Dos muertos, tres heridos y tres secuestrados tras ataque de colonos a comunidades indígenas de Waspam. *La Prensa* 18 December http://www.laprensa.com.ni/2015/12/18/departamentales/1956617-nuevo-enfrentamiento-entre-colonos-e-indigenas (Accessed 27 January 2015).

Romero E (2015c) Daniel Ortega sale en defensa de Samir Matamoros. *La Prensa* 10 September http://www.laprensa.com.ni/2015/09/10/nacionales/1899085-ortega-sale-en-defensa-de-samir (Accessed 27 January 2015).

Romero E (2016a) Ejército de Nicaragua confirma adquisición de 50 tanques rusos. *La Prensa* 25 April http://www.laprensa.com.ni/2016/04/25/nacionales/2024716-nicargua-recibira-50-tanques-rusos (Accessed 8 June 2016).

Romero E (2016b) Arrestan por una hora a feministas en protesta. *La Prensa* 28 September http://www.laprensa.com.ni/2016/09/28/nacionales/2108103-arrestan-por-una-hora-a-feministas-en-protesta (Accessed 12 December 2016).

Romero E, Garth J and Álvarez L (2015) Gobierno niega crisis indígena ante CIDH. *La Prensa* 22 October http://www.laprensa.com.ni/2015/10/22/departamentales/1923376-gobierno-niega-crisis-indigena-ante-cidh (Accessed 28 November 2015).

Romero E, Álvarez R and Moncada R (2015) Orteguismo hizo de todo y no pudo. *La Prensa* 28 October http://www.laprensa.com.ni/2015/10/28/nacionales/1926674-orteguismo-hizo-de-todo-y-no-pudo (Accessed 1 December 2015).

Rowe W and Schelling V (1991) *Memory and Modernity: Popular Culture in Latin America.* London: Verso.

Sáenz E (2015) Las cuentas de Firuliche. [Blog] *Enrique Sáenz.* http://enriquesaenz.com/2015/11/04/las-cuentas-de-firuliche/ (Accessed 14 November 2015).

Sáenz E (2016) Un año amargo en el campo internacional para Ortega. *Confidencial* 11 January http://confidencial.com.ni/un-ano-amargo-en-el-campo-internacional-para-ortega/ (Accessed 1 March 2016).

Sáenz M (2000) Dussel on Marx: Living labor and the materiality of life. In L M Alcoff and L Mendieta (eds) *Thinking from the Underside of History: Enrique Dussel's Philosophy of Liberation.* Lanham: Rowman and Littlefield, pp. 213–248.

Salinas Maldonado C (2014) ¿Por qué se calla, Comandante Ortega? *El País* 22 January http://internacional.elpais.com/internacional/2014/01/22/actualidad/1390352905_814181.html (Accessed 4 March 2016).

Salinas Maldonado C (2015) Nicaragua, el 'Gran Canal'y la perpetuación de Daniel Ortega. *El País* 1 January http://internacional.elpais.com/internacional/2015/01/01/actualidad/1420148520_749810.html (Accessed 14 September 2015).

Salinas Maldonado C (2016) Ortega confirma su giro autoritario al nombrar a su esposa candidata a vicepresidenta. *El País* 3 August http://internacional.elpais.com/internacional/2016/08/03/america/1470183782_674749.html (Accessed 7 August 2016).

Schmidt B (2011) Nicaragua's president rules airwaves to control image. *New York Times* 28 November http://www.nytimes.com/2011/11/29/world/americas/daniel-ortega-extends-control-to-nicaraguas-airwaves.html (Accessed 2 November 2015).

Schneider K (2015) Nicaragua canal environmental assessment criticized as scientifically weak, technically inadequate. *Circle of Blue* 5 June http://www.circleofblue.org/waternews/2015/world/nicaragua-canal-environmental-assessment-criticized-as-scientifically-weak-technically-inadequate/ (Accessed 24 January 2016).

Schiwy F (2009) *Indianizing Film: Decolonization, the Andes, and the Question of Technology.* Piscataway: Rutgers University Press.

Semana (2016) Daniel Ortega: De guerrillero a dictador *Semana* 6 August http://linkis.com/www.semana.com/mundo/dx3cB (Accessed 7 August 2016).

Shifman L (2012) An anatomy of a YouTube meme. *New Media and Society* 14(2): 187–203.

Shifman L (2014) *Memes in Digital Culture.* Cambridge, MA: The MIT Press, Kindle edition.

Silva J A (2015) Claves para entender el conflicto en el Caribe Norte. *La Prensa* 17 September http://www.laprensa.com.ni/2015/09/17/reportajes-especiales/1903452-claves-para-entender-el-conflicto-en-el-caribe-norte (Accessed 14 November 2015).

Silva J A (2016) Nicaragua entre los más corruptos. *La Prensa* 28 January http://www.laprensa.com.ni/2016/01/28/nacionales/1976620-nicaragua-los-mas-corruptos (Accessed 2 February 2016).

Slater T (2012) The myth of "Broken Britain": Welfare reform and the production of ignorance. *Antipode* 46(4): 948–969.

Smith A (2011) Nicaragua's slip back to authoritarianism. *Global Public Square* 10 November http://globalpublicsquare.blogs.cnn.com/2011/11/10/nicaraguas-slip-back-to-authoritarianism/ (Accessed 4 March 2016).

Snickars P and Vonderau P (2009) Introduction. In P Snickars and P Vonderau (eds) *The YouTube Reader.* Stockholm: National Library of Sweden, pp. 9–21.

Sociedad Interamericana de Prensa (1994) Declaración de Chapultepec. Available at http://www.sipiapa.org/contenidos/acerca-de-la-declaracion.html (Accessed 8 November 2015).

Strangelove M (2015). *Post-TV: Piracy, Cord-Cutting, and the Future of Television.* Toronto: University of Toronto Press.

Terranova T (2004). *Network Culture: Politics for the Information Age.* London: Pluto Press.

Téllez D M (2015) Ortega sin pasamontañas [Facebook status] 5 September https://www.facebook.com/photo.php?fbid=10207775846339378&set=a.1619551813935.2090153.1390594446&type=1 (Accessed 9 September 2015).

The Late Late Show with James Corden (2016) What Men Do for Love [YouTube] 4 August https://www.youtube.com/watch?v=XH1kbHP_N3E (Accessed 7 August 2016).

Thompson J B (2005) The new visibility. *Theory, Culture and Society* 22(6): 31–51.

Trolleando a Daniel Ortega (2015) un juventud sandinista es el vivo ejemplo de la ignorancia que reina en estos chavalos pendejos [Facebook video] 30 October https://www.facebook.com/1475910909297740/videos/1742351392653689/ (Accessed 1 December 2015).

Trouillot M R (1995) *Silencing the Past: Power and the Production of History.* Boston: Beacon.

Tuchman G (1978) The symbolic annihilation of women by the mass media. In G Tuchman, A Daniels and J Benet (Eds) *Hearth and Home: Images of Women in Mass Media.* New York: Oxford University Press, pp. 3–38.

Turner, T. 1992. Defiant images: The Kayapo appropriation of video. *Anthropology Today* 8(6): 5–16.

United Nations Special Rapporteur (2015) Nicaragua communications: May 1, 2011 to February 28, 2015 http://freeassembly.net/reports/nicaragua-communications/ (Accessed 3 March 2016).

Univisión Noticias (2015) Carlos Chamorro: "Daniel Ortega se ha consolidado porque ha hecho fraude electoral" [YouTube] 18 October https://www.youtube.com/watch?v=OsyPkepu6bc (Accessed 19 November 2015).

Vílchez D (2015) Censura policial, ataque a la libertad de prensa. *Confidencial* 26 October http://confidencial.com.ni/censura-policial-ataque-a-la-libertad-de-prensa/ (Accessed 27 October 2016).

Villareal R (2017a) Guillotina por participar en acto con Sergio Ramírez. *La Prensa 3* March http://www.laprensa.com.ni/2017/03/03/politica/2192000-guillotina-por-participar-en-acto-con-sergio-ramirez (Accessed 31 March 2017).

Villareal R (2017b) FSLN destituye a concejal de San Juan del Sur por tomarse foto con Laura Dogu. *La Prensa* 29 March http://www.laprensa.com.ni/2017/03/29/departamentales/2207099-fsln-destituye-a-concejal-de-san-juan-del-sur-por-tomarse-foto-con-laura-dogu (Accessed 31 March 2017).

Villareal R and Silva J A (2016) Ortega ha destituido 33 alcaldes desde 2008 en Nicaragua. *La Prensa* 21 January http://www.laprensa.com.ni/2016/01/21/politica/1972954-ortega-ha-destituido-33-ediles-desde-el-2008 (Accessed 23 January 2016).

vivanicaragua13 (2015) Caribe Sur celebra 28 años de autonomía [YouTube] 31 October https://www.youtube.com/watch?v=-cZfZAKLLiI (Accessed 26 November 2015).

Wade P (1997) *Race and Ethnicity in Latin America.* London: Pluto Press.

Wade L (2016) A nation divided. *Science* 351(6270): 220–223.

Watts M (2003) Development and governmentality. *Singapore Journal of Tropical Geography* 24 (1): 6–34.

Weatherford E (1990) Native visions: The growth of indigenous media. *Aperture* 119: 58–61.

Williams-Guillén K, Álvarez P, Covich A, Huete-Pérez J, Crowl T, Stoa R and Briceño H (2015) Nicaragua's mega canal could become a mega mistake without a sound scientific basis [press release] 15 June http://sercweb.fiu.edu/helpful-link/news/2015/nicaraguas-mega-canal-could-become-mega-mistake/ (Accessed 17 November 2015).

Wilson P (2015) Indigenous media: Linking the local, translocal, global and virtual. In S Mains, J Cupples and C Lukinbeal (eds) *Mediated Geographies and Geographies of Media.* Dordrecht: Springer, pp. 367–384.

Wilson P and Stewart M (eds) (2008) *Global Indigenous Media: Cultures, Poetics and Politics.* Durham: Duke University Press.

Zibechi R (2010) *Dispersing Power: Social Movements as Anti-State Forces.* Oakland: AK Press.

Zibechi R (2012) *Territories in Resistance: A Cartography of Latin American Social Movements.* Oakland: AK Press.

Zoad Mendoza T (2016) Colonos secuestran, matan y violan a indígenas. *La Prensa* 31 January http://www.laprensa.com.ni/2016/01/31/nacionales/1978204-colonos-secuestran-matan-y-violan-a-indigenas (Accessed 12 December 2016).

MIX
Papier aus verantwortungsvollen Quellen
Paper from responsible sources
FSC® C105338

If you have any concerns about our products,
you can contact us on
ProductSafety@springernature.com

In case Publisher is established outside the EU,
the EU authorized representative is:
Springer Nature Customer Service Center GmbH
Europaplatz 3, 69115 Heidelberg, Germany

Printed by Libri Plureos GmbH
in Hamburg, Germany